INSIGHT

Biblical Inspiration For Daily Living

TEMI ODEJIDE

ISBN: 978-1-9160682-2-3

DEDICATION

To every lover of the Bible who desires a deeper walk with God.

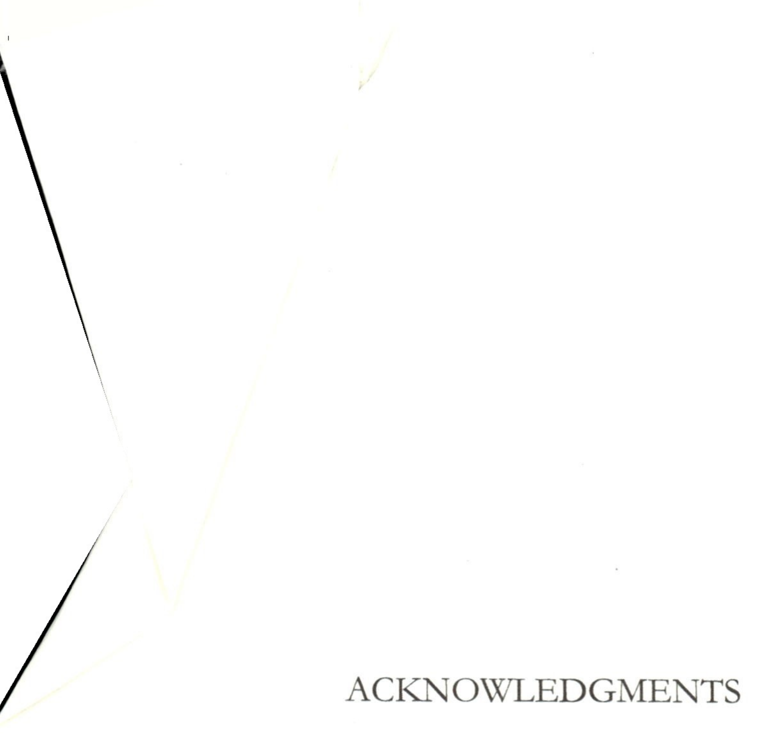

ACKNOWLEDGMENTS

To all the key persons that worked behind the scenes to see this devotional come to realization.

ABOUT THE AUTHOR

Temi Odejide is a medical doctor turned teacher and preacher of God's Word. His core passion, since his youth, is the demystifying of truth, to bring it into practical application, in day-to-day living. He is a man of many parts, but his teaching gift excels above others. He is a pastor, teacher, preacher, motivational speaker, author, leadership expert, life coach, mentor, forward navigation strategist and much more. He is the serving Resident Pastor of House on the Rock, London. He is happily married to Abisoye and they have three wonderful children.

Follow him on Instagram and Twitter @temiodejide
And on Facebook @DrTemiOdejide

Visit his website @ www.temiodejide.com
To give feedback, make comments or share testimonies, email
temilolu.odejide@gmail.com

PREFACE TO INSIGHT

Insight is to have a clear or deep perception of a situation; a feeling of understanding; the clear (and often sudden) understanding of a complex situation; grasping the inner nature of things intuitively. Insight is really about understanding.

Too often, the Bible seems to be this mystical book that is so hard to understand, but that should not be the case. My mantra has been demystifying of truth – I seek to make the complex simple. This insight devotional is a collection of 366 devotional articles that are tailored to give insight into the revelations in God's Word.

2 Timothy 2:15 in the original King James translation says *'Study to shew thyself approved unto God, a workman that needeth not to be ashamed, rightly dividing the word of truth.'* We cannot be approved in any area without studying. So also, we cannot be approved in our various life situations as believers in the Bible without study. In developing this devotional I have made assiduous effort to 'rightly divide the word of truth' without losing the multilayered revelations that abound therein. This devotional is designed to truly give you insight and get you studying, even further.

October 1

UPGRADE

Pilot Text: '...And the first voice which I heard was like a trumpet... saying, "Come up here...' – Revelations 4:1

God is calling you to come up higher. To come up higher is to upgrade. It is time to upgrade. To upgrade is to go to the next level. But to upgrade, there are some things you have to do.

Typically, for an upgrade to happen, there has to be an exchange. You have to make an exchange. Exchange your weakness for His strength. Your poverty for His wealth. Your confusion for His direction. Your pain for His gain.

Typically, for an upgrade to happen, there has to be a trade; you trade in the old for the new. You have to make a trade. Trade in the old things for some new things. Trade in your sorrows for His joy. Trade in your fear for His faith. Trade in your doubt for unwavering confidence. Trade in your negative attitude for a positive faith-filled attitude.

For an upgrade to happen, there has to be a letting go. Let go of the old and embrace the new thing that God is doing. You can't hold unto the last level and go to the next level at the same time. You have to let go of the last level to go to the next level. There are things you have to let go of to be able to go to the next level. Abram had to let go of Lot to be able to go to his next level. He could not take Lot along with him into his next level. There are some things, some people and some relationships that you can't take into your next level or you will forfeit going into your next level.

To upgrade, exchange, trade in and let go to, today.

Key Thought: God wants to take us to a new level of relationship with Him. Let go of the old and embrace the new.
Intelligent Prayer Point: Pray that God will help you to open your mind into new realms of revelation in Him.
Support Scriptures: Proverbs 15:24, Isaiah 60:1 & 2 Peter 3:18

October 2

UPGRADE TO UPGRADE

Pilot Text: '…And the first voice which I heard… saying, "Come up here…' – Revelations 4:1

God is calling you higher to the next level. He wants to bring an upgrade into your life. But to upgrade, you must upgrade. What do I mean by this?

The promise and prophecy of upgrade is often associated with material and financial upgrades. That is not incorrect but it is incomplete.

You have heard it said that 'water seeks its own level'. This is so true in the business world and generally in life and it means high quality finds high quality and low quality finds low quality. To be upgraded is to go to another higher level than where you are. But to remain at that new level, you have to have gotten ready for the new level or you would be demoted to the level that your character and competence can truly handle. So, you must upgrade before you can upgrade.

The spiritual controls the physical. So, enduring physical upgrades are preceded by spiritual upgrades. So, a spiritual upgrade is essential. You have to upgrade your prayer life. You cannot pray at the level you have been praying and expect to go to another level. Your prayer goes first to where you want to go.

You have to upgrade your word study. The word is the source of all things. You can only rise to the level of your revelation. You have to labor in the word to go to the next level.

You have to upgrade your worship and service. It is the aroma of sincere worship and faithful service that attracts the lifting of the Lord.

You have to upgrade your giving. The measure used to give back unto you, is your measure. You determine the harvest by the seed sown. You have to give at the new level to go to the new level.

You have to upgrade to upgrade. Are you ready to upgrade?

Key Thought: Personal spiritual upgrade precedes life upgrade.
Intelligent Prayer Point: Pray for the commitment to upgrade your spiritual life.
Support Scriptures: Mark 4:24, Ephesians 4:23 & 2 Timothy 2:15

October 3

iOS and Apps

Pilot Text: '...no one puts new wine into old wineskins; or else the new wine will burst the wineskins and be spilled, and the wineskins will be ruined.' – Luke 5:37

We are still talking about upgrading. God wants to upgrade you.

Every now and then Apple decides that it wants to go to a totally new level. When any mobile company wants to make a significant shift upwards, there are some changes that must take place. Minor shifts often only involve updates to the existing systems, but when it's a major shift, there is a total upgrade of the iOS – intelligent Operating System. Why? Because what they want to be able to download to you, the old iOS cannot carry (old wine skins cannot hold new wine).

For the upgrade that God wants to bring into your life, there has to be a total upgrade of your current iOS – intelligent Operating System.
But when a major upgrade is coming, it is not just the iOS that is upgraded, the Apps also get updates to make them compatible with the new iOS; these updates are upgrades.
So, it is not just your spiritual iOS that needs to be upgraded but all your Apps. Apps are applications. Your spiritual Apps are the ways you apply God's word to your life.

For a true upgrade, you have to upgrade your iOS – intelligent Operating System. The way you operate with God. Your walk with God has to go to another level of intimacy. But also your applications must go to another level – the way you apply God's word to your life. Stop limiting God's word to only certain religious areas of your life and start to apply the word of God across board because it speaks to every area of life.

God has so much He wants to download into your life but you must upgrade your iOS and your spiritual Apps today.

Key Thought: Upgrade your iOS and Apps to upgrade your life.
Intelligent Prayer Point: Pray to rightly apply God's Word to your life for upgrades.
Support Scriptures: Proverbs 23:7, 1 Corinthians 13:11 & James 1:22-25

October 6

LOOK UP TO GO UP

Pilot Text: 'After these things I looked, and behold, a doors standing open in heaven. And the… voice… saying, "Come up here…' – Revelations 4:1

When John looked up, he saw a door standing open in heaven. The door was not going to be opened; it was not being opened, it was already open. This is a prophetic word for someone. The door is already open. It's already done. It's already settled. It's already sorted.

The door is already open. But it was open on a level that John was not yet. John had to look up to be able to even see the open door. The Bible uses the word - 'behold' which means to look with the intent to see. Just as John had to look up with intent to see, so you will have to look up with intent to see in order to go up. You have to look up to go up.

Your upgrade is connected to where and what you are looking at, because you will ultimately go where you are looking. You can't go up while looking down. The problem sometimes is that you have been looking in all the wrong places.
Looking back at your losses. Looking down at your failures. Looking around for the help of man. It is time to look up, to go up.

Looking up also speaks to how you think – 'For as he thinks in his heart, so is he…' – Proverbs 23:7. Your thought life controls your real life. You cannot rise, sustainably, above the level of your thoughts. Water seeks its own level. Your life will always recalibrate itself to the level of your thoughts. You have to elevate your thoughts out of impossibility into possibility thinking.

To upgrade today, LOOK UP TO GO UP!

Key Thought: You go in the direction that you look. So, look up.
Intelligent Prayer Point: Pray that your eyes be opened that you might see doors that are already open for you.
Support Scriptures: Psalms 119:18, Psalms 121:1 & Proverbs 23:7

October 7

COMMITTED TO UPGRADE

Pilot Text: 'Therefore He says: "Awake, you who sleep, arise from the dead, and Christ will give you light' – Ephesians 5:14

He was due for an upgrade. His contract date had arrived. He was elated because the latest iPhone X had just been released. He could hardly wait to get his hands on it. He hadn't been able to get it, first thing in the morning, lest he be late for work (though he considered embracing the consequences of lateness with the pleasure of holding the phone, but thought better of it). It was lunch break and off he went to the phone shop down the street. He skipped out of the shop a few minutes later with the phone in his hand for nothing. But was it really for nothing? All he had to do was renew his contract with them.

The carrier did not upgrade him for nothing. They gave him the upgrade on the premise of his recommitment to another term contract. A commitment precedes an upgrade.

In spite of the many years that he had been with that carrier they were not giving him an upgrade solely on the premise of his history but rather because of his continued future loyalty to them. He could not argue that because I have been with you so long you should give me the upgrade with no commitment from me. Every upgrade is premised on commitment.

If you want an upgrade you have to be ready to pay the price of commitment and recommitment.

God will meet you at the level of your commitment. How committed are you to upgrade? Anyone that goes higher has made more commitment, more sacrifice, more loyalty and more investment. The greater your level of commitment the greater your upgrade.

Key Thought: Commitment precedes upgrades.
Intelligent Prayer Point: Pray for the grace required to do the needful for the actualization of the promise.
Support Scriptures: Romans 6:13, Philippians 2:12-13 & James 1:22-25

October 8

MEMORY CAPACITY

Pilot Text: '…no one puts new wine into old wineskins; or else the new wine will burst the wineskins and be spilled, and the wineskins will be ruined.' – Luke 5:37

God has an upgrade for you, but He cannot download it to you till you have upgraded your iOS (intelligent Operating System) and Apps (applications) to be able to handle it. He won't pour His new wine into old wineskins, lest both the new wine and the wineskins be lost. I hope you have embarked on the upgrading process of your iOS and Apps since you caught this revelation.

I recently found out that some applications would still not work properly even though your iOS has been upgraded if you don't have sufficient free memory to run them. So, sometimes, you've upgraded your iOS and updated your apps, but still, things are not working properly… because you don't have sufficient memory capacity to operate.

Your memory is clogged with all sorts of redundant memories, remnants of passed processes and even old applications that you are no longer using. It is time to free up your memory capacity. Clear out the junk.

Some powerful high definition applications need more memory than others to operate. So, your memory capacity is essential for operating on an upgraded level.

David faced an 'upgraded' Goliath by tapping into his memory of victory over the lion and the bear. So, an expanded memory capacity is not all about a blank memory but a selective memory that recalls the promises and testimonies of the Lord.

Will you upgrade your memory capacity to recall the faithfulness of the Lord to operate on a totally new level? Upgrade today!

Key Thought: Upgrade your faith by recalling the faithfulness of God.
Intelligent Prayer Point: Pray to always remember the faithfulness of God even when faced with challenging situations.
Support Scriptures: Psalms 20:7, 77:11, 103:2, & 1 Chronicles 16:12

October 9

DON'T BE SILENT

Pilot Text: 'And since we have the same spirit of faith, according to what is written, "I believed and therefore I spoke," we also believe and therefore speak.' – 2 Corinthians 4:13

Faith speaks. Faith does not keep quiet. Faith isn't silent. Faith speaks. We believe, therefore we speak. If we truly believe, we would speak. If we don't speak, then maybe we don't truly believe.

With the heart, man believes unto righteousness and with the mouth confession is made unto salvation. Through the belief of the heart, we align with heavenly truths and through the confession of the mouth, from a believing heart, heavenly truths are translated into our world. Don't be silent. Faith speaks.

What does faith speak? '…God, who gives life to the dead, and calls those things that be not as though they were.' – Romans 4:17. Faith calls things into being. What have you been calling lately? Faith is a caller.

Consider what Faith calls, but also, what Faith does not call.
Faith calls WHAT IS NOT as though it were.
Faith does not call WHAT IS as though it were not.

Faith does not deny reality; it simply embraces an alternative reality. Faith is not into denial of what is wrong, but into approval of what is right and desired. Faith does not lie about what is happening, it speaks what it wants to happen.
This is a fine point and a vital one.
I don't deny my present reality, but I keep at work on actualizing the reality my faith sees. Faith does not reinforce the negative that already exists by continually rehearsing it, but beckons the positive it wants, by persistently calling it. Don't let situations and circumstances shut your mouth. Don't let the devil steal your voice.

Key Thought: Faith is not silent. Faith speaks things into being.
Intelligent Prayer Point: Pray for the spirit of faith to possess you and that you continually speak the words of faith.
Support Study Scriptures: Ecclesiastes 3:7, Matthew 17:20 & Mark 11:13,14,20

October 10

DON'T FORGET WHAT YOU SAW IN THE MIRROR

Pilot Text: 'But we all, with unveiled face, beholding as in a mirror the glory of the Lord, are being transformed into the same image from glory to glory, just as by the Spirit of the Lord.' – 2 Corinthians 3:18

We know that upon salvation, we are instantaneously transformed in our spirit, but we must renew our minds, continually, to allow the inner transformation subdue the outward conformity. We must continually look into the mirror of God's Word to be transformed into the image of glory that we see. The Word of God is the mirror.

James 1:23-25 illustrates that the hearer of the word that does not do it, is like a man that looks in the mirror (the Word of God), sees how he looks but once he turns away from it, he forgets what he saw and as a result loses his blessing. So, hearing or seeing the Word is not enough because forgetfulness would still set in. And the image you forget you cannot be transformed into. But by hearing and doing, you are delivered from spiritual forgetfulness.

So, we must commit to constantly looking into the mirror of God's Word to hear and see who we are, in Him, and then, do what we hear and see.

I look in the mirror and I see myself delivered. I look in the mirror and I see myself free. I look in the mirror and I see myself living the abundant life. I look in the mirror and I see myself above and not beneath. I look in the mirror and I see myself as head and not the tail. I look in the mirror and I see myself more than a conqueror. I look in the mirror and I see myself roar.

Do you look in the mirror? What do you see? Don't forget what you see in the mirror.

Key Thought: You become what you focus on, focus on the Word.
Intelligent Prayer Point: Ask the help of the Holy Spirit in allowing an inner transformation to subdue the outward conformity, as you dig deep into God's Word.
Support Scriptures: Psalms 119:105,133, Proverbs 4:4 & Luke 11:28

October 11

GET INTO THE DEEP END

Pilot Text: 'Deep calls unto deep at the noise of your waterspouts: all your waves and your billows are gone over me'. – Psalms 42:5

I learnt to swim late. But before I learnt to swim, I was scared of the deep end. I preferred to stay in the shallow end. But every once in a while, I would venture to the middle of the pool to feign some pseudo-proficiency in swimming, as long as my feet were still firmly touching the floor of the pool. Once I could not feel the bottom of the pool, I would panic and rush back towards the shallow end as quickly as I could.

Why are we scared of the deep, before we can swim? Obviously, because we are afraid of drowning. But maybe more accurately, because we are afraid of losing control. As long as my feet are still touching the floor of the pool, I am in control, but once I lose that connection, I lose control.

Even the meekest of us like being in control. We feel safe when we are in control. We think we can determine the outcome when we are in control. This is why we are slow to submit to authority, because we know that with that submission is a measure of loss of control.

Yet, it is in the deep end that our breakthrough waits. It is time to dive into the deep end. The deep end is where you are no longer in control and He is fully in control. Let go and let God!

'When my heart is overwhelmed; lead me to the Rock that is higher than I.' – Psalms 61:2. If your heart is overwhelmed it is time to get into the deep. The Rock that is higher than you is the deep end.

Today relinquish control to Christ, let Him take control. LET GO AND LET GOD!

Key Thought: You have to relinquish control to God, to enter the blessing.
Intelligent Prayer Point: Ask God for help in relinquishing absolute control to Him, not just in words, but in deed.
Support Scriptures: Proverbs 3:5,6, Proverbs 16:9 & 2 Thessalonians 3:5

October 12

GIVE ME AN ANCHOR

Pilot Text: 'Which hope we have as an anchor of the soul, both sure and steadfast, and which entered into that within the veil' – Hebrews 6:19

I don't know about you, but I need an anchor for my soul. To say that we live in challenging times is an understatement. I'm in a flux. The winds are blowing. The waves are rising. The billows are roaring. Contradictions are staring me in the face. I have the promise, but I'm experiencing the opposite. More bills than money to pay. Between a rock and a hard place. Pressed on every side. Juggling so many balls. I NEED AN ANCHOR!

An anchor is a mechanical device that prevents a vessel from moving, a central cohesive source of support and stability, to fix firmly and stably, to secure a vessel, to stabilize… I NEED AN ANCHOR!

Hope is an anchor for your soul. Hope is a sure picture of a preferred future. Hope keeps your soul stable in the midst of the storm because you know that after the storm, you are coming out on top. So you have to keep hope alive. You have to keep believing.

This hope that is an anchor for our soul is both sure and steadfast and has entered into that within the veil. What does this mean? This hope has gone ahead. HE HAS GONE AHEAD! He went beyond the veil. He has gone beyond what you can see. Nothing that is happening now is taking Him by surprise.

Let this be an anchor for your soul. Christ in you the hope of glory. He has gone ahead. He has gone beyond what you know, have seen or have experienced, nothing is taking Him by surprise. So, peace be still.

I'VE GOT AN ANCHOR FOR MY SOUL. WHAT ABOUT YOU?

Key Thought: Christ is our hope and the anchor for our soul.
Intelligent Prayer Point: Pray that the revelation of Christ in you will be an enduring anchor for your soul.
Support Scriptures: Jer. 17:7, Rom. 5:5, Rom. 8:25 & Col. 1:27

October 13

GOD WANTS TO BLESS YOU

Pilot Text: '…I will make you a great nation; I will bless you and make your name great; and you shall be a blessing. I will bless those who bless you and I will curse him who curses you; and in you all the families of the earth shall be blessed'. – Genesis 12:2,3

THIS IS DEFINITELY A COVENANT OF BLESSING. This is Abraham's blessing. Our God is a God of blessing and His divine intention has always been to bless.

After creating man and before His first instructions to man to be fruitful, multiply, fill the earth and subdue it, Genesis 1:28 says He, first, blessed them. The blessing came first. This establishes that God's intention has always been to bless. The blessing had to come first because it is the empowerment to prosper. IT IS A COVENANT OF BLESSING!

This covenant of blessing spanned through the generations all the way even into the New Testament where, in Galatians 3:13,14 it says: 'Christ has redeemed us from the curse of the law, being made a curse for us: for it is written, cursed is every one that hangs on a tree: THAT THE BLESSING OF ABRAHAM might come on the Gentiles through Jesus Christ…' And in verse 29 it says 'And if you be Christ's, then are you Abraham's seed, and heirs according to the promise'. IF YOU ARE CHRIST'S, YOU ARE ABRAHAM'S SEED. Abraham's blessings are yours. In Christ, I can appropriate every blessing of Abraham. That means: He will make me a great nation, He will bless me and make my name great; and I will be a blessing…

God's intent is not just to bless me, but to make me a source of blessing. Wow! I am blessing dynamo. I set up cycles of blessing wherever I go. ANYONE THAT BLESSES ME SHALL BE BLESSED. But there is a reverse side of the blessing: ANYONE THAT CURSES ME SHALL BE CURSED! Walk in the consciousness of your covenant of blessing with God today and always.

Key Thought: God always starts with the blessing.
Intelligent Prayer Point: Pray to function from the mind of Christ; a blessed mindset.
Support Scriptures: Genesis 1:28, Malachi 3:12; Galatians 3:9 & Eph. 1:3

October 14

WHEN ARE YOU GOING TO BLESS ME?

Pilot Text: '…I will make you a great nation; I will bless you and make your name great; and you shall be a blessing. I will bless those who bless you and I will curse him who curses you; and in you all the families of the earth shall be blessed'. – Genesis 12:2,3

My Challenge is not with God's willingness to bless me. I know His divine intent to bless me beyond comprehension. My problem is not with His ability to bless me. He is Omnipotent. He is more than able to bless me. My challenge is with WHEN He chooses to bless me. My problem is with His chosen timing for my blessing.

Ecclesiastes 3:11 – He makes all things beautiful in His time… I wish it was my time and not His time because His time seems to take so long. When are you going to bless me? And then too often He chooses to bless in the midst of a storm.

But, Ephesians 1:3 says, 'Blessed be the God and Father of our Lord Jesus Christ, who has blessed us with ALL spiritual blessings in heavenly places in Christ' From this Scripture you understand that YOU ARE ALREADY BLESSED. Hallelujah! I am ALREADY BLESSED! I'VE GOT THE BLESSING!

However, there are two clauses in this scripture: the blessings are spiritual blessings and they are in heavenly places. So, I have got to learn how to transfer the blessings from the spiritual realm into my physical realm. I have got to learn how to move the blessings from heavenly places into my earthly places. But it starts with me accepting, acknowledging and believing that I have ALREADY BEEN BLESSED!
So, the question of 'when' is past. I AM ALREADY BLESSED!

Go out into your day, today, with the confidence that you are already blessed! GO WITH THE BLESSING!

Key Thought: You are already blessed, its manifestation is just a matter of time.
Intelligent Prayer Point: God is never late, pray for patience to enter and bask in your blessing.
Support Scriptures: Psalms 31:15, Malachi 3:12, Galatians 3:9 & Eph. 1:3

October 15

WHY DO YOU WAIT TO BLESS ME IN THE STORM?

Pilot Text: '…I will make you a great nation; I will bless you and make your name great; and you shall be a blessing. I will bless those who bless you and I will curse him who curses you; and in you all the families of the earth shall be blessed'. – Genesis 12:2,3

The truth is that most of the time the translation of the blessings from the spiritual realm and heavenly places into my world takes time. It seems God waits to bless me…in the storm. Ever felt like that?

Why does He wait for Lazarus to be dead 4 days before He shows up? Why does He wait for me to be facing the red sea with the chariots of Egypt behind before He intervenes? Why does He wait for all hell to break loose before He unveils His delivering hand? GOD, WHY DO YOU WAIT TO BLESS ME IN THE STORM?

The first reason is:
God uses situations to give you revelation. God uses the storm to unveil Himself to you. Your knowledge of God prior to the stormy situation is mostly intellectual, but God wants to bring you into experiential knowledge of Him. So, He allows the situation to unveil Him to you.

You do not really know Him as healer till you have been sick. You do not really know Him as deliverer till you have been captive. You do not really know Him as provider till you have been in lack.

So, God uses the stormy situation to experientially unveil another aspect of His character. Martha, Mary and Lazarus could not really know Christ as the resurrection and the life till Lazarus died.

The second reason is:
God is a God of contrast. Contrast is the act of distinguishing by comparing difference. It is for contrast that diamonds are displayed on black background so the contrast amplifies the beauty of the diamonds. The contrast of the night sky causes us to appreciate the light of the stars. So, God uses the contrast of your storm to bring focus on His attributes.

So, your storm is a SET-UP for God to SHOW UP! HE IS JEHOVAH EL-CONTRASTE!

So, I dance in the storm because I know that Jehovah *El-Contraste* is about to show up! ANYBODY DANCING WITH ME?

Key Thought: Your storms and contradictions are the contrast that God uses to unveil more of Himself to you.
Intelligent Prayer Point: Pray that your gaze will not shift from God, even in the storm.
Support Scriptures: Isaiah 46:10, Psalms 31:15, Malachi 3:12, 2 Corinthians 4:7 & Ephesians 1:3

October 16

STORMS, FAMINES AND EGYPT

Pilot Text: 'And there was a famine in the land…And the Lord…said, Go not down into Egypt; dwell in the land…Then Isaac sowed in that land, and received in the same year an hundredfold: and the Lord blessed him.' – Genesis 26:1,12

Isaac's storm was the famine in the land.
A famine represents lack, not enough, insufficiency, insecurity, inadequacy, loneliness, need, incompetence, deficiency…
What is the logical response to a storm of famine? The reasonable response to a famine is to relocate to where there is water. It was logical for Isaac to relocate to Egypt. Have you ever felt like relocating? But God's instruction to Isaac was "DO NOT GO DOWN TO EGYPT", stay in the land.

Egypt represents the flesh, the emotions and the Devil.
So, when God says "Do not go down to Egypt", what is He really saying to us? He is saying, "don't yield to the temptations of your flesh". "Don't move by emotions". "Don't embrace the negative feelings the storm is throwing at you". "Don't yield to the temptations of the devil". "Don't go down to the carnal way of thinking and doing". "Don't give room to bitterness". "Don't entertain resentfulness". "Don't make permanent decisions based on temporary circumstances".

What is most important in a storm of famine, is to find the Word of the Lord. What is the Lord really saying to you? If He says "stay in the Land", stay in the land. If He says "move", move. The key is WHAT ARE THE INSTRUCTIONS OF THE LORD? What do you believe the Lord is telling you to do? Obey in faith. God has made provision for you even in the storm. His provision is in His Word. FIND AND OBEY HIS WORD!

DON'T GO DOWN TO EGYPT, STAY IN THE WORD!

Key Thought: Obedience is key to your harvest.
Intelligent Prayer Point: Pray for the grace to hear and obey the instructions of the Lord
Support Scriptures: 1 Samuel 15:22, Joshua 1:8 & Proverbs 7:24,25

October 17

SOWING IN FAMINE

Pilot Text: 'And there was a famine in the land…Then Isaac sowed in that land, and received in the same year an hundredfold...' – Genesis 26:1,12

Isaac did not just stay in the land, he sowed in the land. Isaac sowed into the land of famine. Isaac sowed in the midst of his storm. In a time of famine, the land is barren. Yet Isaac sowed into barren land. In famine, seeds are precious and scarce. Isaac took the precious seeds and sowed them in barren land. This was a major risk and great sacrifice. WHY, ISAAC, WHY?

What made Isaac so confident to sow in famine? Where did Isaac's confidence lie? It could not have been in the land, because it was barren and unyielding. It could not have been in the heavens because they were giving no rain. It could not have been in the rivers, because they had dried up. The only thing left for Isaac to have confidence in was the seed.

Isaac was confident in his seed. He believed his wonder seed would produce no matter the conditions. What seed was this that Isaac believed in so? It was the seed of God's Word.

When you sow the seed of God's Word, even in famine, it will still produce. It is the incorruptible seed. It is the original seed. 'For so shall the word be that goes forth from His mouth, it shall not return unto Him void, But it shall accomplish what He pleases and it will prosper in the thing for which He sent it' – Isaiah 55:11

In famine, SOW THE SEED OF GOD'S WORD.
When Isaac's seed hit the barren soil, with no water, it nourished itself and produced a hundred-fold return. SOW THE SEED OF GOD'S WORD IN YOUR HEART, OBEY GOD'S WORD AND WATCH THE HARVEST OVERFLOW!

Key Thought: The real seed that guarantees harvest, even in famine, is the seed of God's Word.
Intelligent Prayer Point: Pray for the grace to always obey the instructions of God's Word.
Support Scriptures: James 1:22; 1 Peter 1:25 & Hebrews 4:12

October 18

IT CANNOT BE DONE OR CAN IT?

Pilot Text: '…whosoever shall say unto this mountain, be removed… and does not doubt…he will have whatever he says'. – Mark 11:23

At the starting place of every great endeavor is found, buried in the sand, the words 'IT CANNOT BE DONE!' Many believed that Mount Everest could not be climbed, but Sir Edmund Hillary and Tenzing Norgay Sherpa, surmounted the peak of Everest in 1953, after many failed attempts by others.

Once, in my youth, I stepped into my father's office and he asked me to run an errand or something and I saw that it clashed with a prior commitment and I replied 'No, I cannot'. He looked up from his table and said 'Never let your first answer be 'No'. There is always a way.' Pause, consider, look at it again and you will start to catch a glimpse of a bypass through which the goal can yet be achieved.

'No' or 'It cannot be done' are dangerous statements to use in the face of challenges or at the introduction of vision. These phrases shut down your creative juices and put a full stop to your forward momentum. When you say "no", you conclude that it is impossible and turn back. Stop, pause, consider, look at it again…

I have the resolute belief that there is always a way. So, in the face of a mountain, I turn not back. I'll either scale it, go round it, dig under it, speak to it or get me some dynamite and blow it out of the way, but, I am not taking "no" for an answer. Let your creative juices flow. It is in the face of seeming impossibility or difficulty that the brightest innovations are born.

To those that would work with me, I say, don't tell me "it cannot be done", rather, ask "how can it be done?" We might have to wait longer, pay more, dig deeper, reach higher but nothing is impossible: THERE IS ALWAYS A WAY. I AM DETERMINED TO FIND MY WAY FORWARD TODAY. WHAT ABOUT YOU?

Key Thought: Nothing is impossible with God.
Intelligent Prayer Point: Ask God for divine strategies to surmount your mountains.
Support Scriptures: Matthew 17:20, Mark 11:23,24 & Luke 1:37

October 19

GOD AND MONEY

Pilot Text: "No servant can serve two masters; for either he will hate the one and love the other, or else he will be loyal to the one and despise the other. You cannot serve God and mammon." – Luke 16:13

This text suggests that the only worthy competitor for God in our hearts is money. This thought is profound. Money can compete with God in your heart. You cannot serve God and money.

We are quick to say we know whom we serve. 'We serve God and not money!' But is this true? Actions speak louder than words.

We come late to Church or not at all once a week, while we are not late once to work during the week come rain or shine. Why? Worship in Church is optional and a matter of convenience, but work is compulsory. [I am not saying that Church is your only avenue of worship, but I am saying that it is your most obvious.] Why is worship in the house of God optional for some, but working the job is not up for debate? The answer is simple. The job is paying you money and you can't joke with that. But what is Church going to give you? **So, are you serving God or money? Just asking…**
But some are first to arrive and last to leave Church, every day of the week but unfaithful in paid employment. What is their drive to the house of God? They hope that somehow, this service would translate to windfalls of money. **So, are they serving God or money? Just asking…**
But it's complicated, because I need money to serve God effectively. So, I must serve God with money.
So, now I am CONFLICTED, because I must work to make money to more effectively serve God, while not allowing money be my primary motivation for my service. This is the delicate balance we must achieve, that we fall not into the trap of serving two masters.

It is time for us (in our actions not just our words) to put God first and LEARN TO SERVE GOD WITH MONEY.

Key Thought: The love of money competes with the love of God. Subdue money by serving God with it.
Intelligent Prayer Point: Pray that the love of money will not invade your heart.
Support Scriptures: Ecclesiastes 5:10, 12:13, 1 Timothy 6:10 & Heb. 13:5

October 20

GOD WANTS TO REVIVE YOU

Pilot Text: "After two days He will revive us..." – Hosea 6:2

God wants to revive you.
To revive is to cause to regain consciousness; to give new life or energy to; to be brought back to life, consciousness or strength; to restore from a depressed, inactive or unused state.
Synonyms for revive include activate, vitalize, reanimate, restore, regenerate, resuscitate, renew…
To revive, is to give life, again.

God wants to revive you. There is no revival without the introduction of life. To introduce life is to revive. Jesus came that we might have life and have it more abundantly. Jesus came to revive us. But, He does not revive the way the world attempts to revive, He revives it better than it was. He replaces the life that you lost with a better life: the life of God. God wants to revive you.

We ask "where is the God of Elijah?" "Where is the God that answers by fire?"
God asks "where are the Elijah's of God?" We say we are waiting on God and God says He is waiting for us.
"Call on me and I will show you great and mighty things which you know not" – Jeremiah 33:3. Where are the callers? He will answer if we call.

God has set the stage to revive, but He responds to what you do. If you call, He will answer. If you seek, He will be found of you. If you knock, He will open the doors. If you ask, He will revive you. Give and He will outgive you. Come and He will come. Move and He will move. God wants to revive you, but needs your action. For every step you take, up the mountain of obedience, God takes a step on the other side of the obedience.

Trigger revival in your life today by your pursuit of God.

Key Thought: God wants to revive you, but needs your cooperation.
Intelligent Prayer Point: Call for revival, now, in your life.
Support Scriptures: 2 Chronicles 7:14, Psalms 62:5 & Amos 3:3

October 21

GOOD MORNING

Pilot Text: "… And the evening and the morning were the first day." – Genesis 1:5

In the midst of the darkness, in the beginning, God was there. Before there was light, God was there. You might not be able to see Him, but He is there. GOD IS IN THE MESS. The Spirit of God moved upon the surface of the deep. GOD IS MOVING IN THE MESS, WORKING OUT A MESSAGE. In the midst of whatever you are going through, GOD IS STILL THERE! He will never leave nor forsake you.

GOD WORKS IN THE DARK.
We would say a whole day is 'day and night'. But in Genesis 1 God repeatedly accounts for a whole day as evening and morning. God starts in the night. God works in the dark.
God is not intimidated by the dark. God is not intimidated by your circumstance. God commands light to shine out of darkness (2 Corinthians 4:6). If God could start in the darkness of nothingness and call all things out of nothing, what is your situation that He cannot handle? God often starts His best work in the dark.
We want Him to start in the light, but He starts in the dark. The dark room: where He turns the negatives into positives. In the dark, you cannot see. You cannot see your potential, power nor possibilities.

In the dark, you cannot see, BUT YOU CAN HEAR!

God wants you to stop depending on what you see and depend only on the Word of God you hear. Faith comes by hearing the Word of God. Keep hearing.

LISTEN! The darkest hour is just before dawn. The night is never forever. Don't die in the dark. Don't quit in the seasons of obscurity and isolation. Don't give up, morning is coming.
"…WEEPING MAY ENDURE FOR A NIGHT, BUT JOY COMES IN THE MORNING." – Psalms 30:5

The greeting 'Good Morning' is not just a greeting, but also a prophetic benediction on the night. So, I say to you "GOOD MORNING!"

GOOD MORNING, THE DOORS ARE OPEN!

Key Thought: Make sure to endure through the night, because morning is coming.
Intelligent Prayer Point: Pray for grace to persevere through the night to the breaking of dawn.
Support Scriptures: Psalms 30:5, Lamentations 3:22,23 & Isaiah 58:8

October 22

GOT THE KEYS

Pilot Text: "…the gates of hell shall not prevail… And I will give you the keys of the kingdom of heaven, and whatever you bind on earth will be bound in heaven, and whatever you loose on earth will be loosed in heaven." – Matthew 16:18,19

The gates of hell will not prevail against a church or life built on Christ. If Christ is the One building you, the gates of hell will not prevail against you. The gates, the strategies, schemes, plans and plots of hell will not prevail against you. Then, Jesus said He would give us the keys (plural not singular) of the kingdom of heaven and authority to bind and loose on earth and it would be done in heaven.

He said He would give us the keys, future tense. He said 'He would' because He had not yet died and risen from the dead. In Revelations 1:18, Jesus said "I am He who lives, and was dead, and behold, I am alive forevermore. Amen. And I have the keys of Hades and of Death." When Jesus died and rose again He took back all the keys. Now that He has risen and lives forever, all authority and power is in His hands and He is no longer going to give us the keys of the kingdom of heaven, through delegation of authority, HE HAS GIVEN US THE KEYS.

You and I now have the keys we just didn't know it.

HE HAS GIVEN US THE KEYS OF THE KINGDOM OF HEAVEN AND WHATEVER YOU BIND ON EARTH WILL BE BOUND IN HEAVEN, AND WHATEVER YOU LOOSE ON EARTH WILL BE LOOSED IN HEAVEN.

Our job now is finding those keys (plural not singular) in the Word of God and using them effectively.

YOU'VE GOT THE KEYS. FIND THEM. USE THEM!

Key Thought: Christ has given us the keys to (RETAIN OUR)all-round victory in life.
Intelligent Prayer Point: Bind every negative things coming against you and loose the favour of God to abound in your life.
Support Study Scriptures: Psalms 149:6-9, Isaiah 22:22 & Mark 3:27

October 23

GRACE DID IT!

Pilot Text: "…This is the word of the Lord… Not by might, nor by power, but by my Spirit…who art thou, O great mountain? Before Zerubbabel thou shalt become a plain: and he shall bring forth the headstone thereof with shoutings, crying, Grace, grace unto it." – Zechariah 4:6,7

O great mountain! Are you facing a mountain right now? The truth is life is often a progression of mountains and valleys. So, even if you are not facing a mountain right now, it is just a matter of time, you will be facing one.

So, what mountain are you facing right now? A mountain of disappointment? A mountain of pain? A mountain of confusion? A mountain of bills? A mountain of discouragement? A mountain of unfulfilled expectations? A mountain of delay? A mountain of opposition? What is your mountain?

Our typical response to our mountains is to look for what we have: our ability, our resources, our competences, our connections, our might or our power. But the truth is, the solution to your mountain is not in might (force or resource) nor in power (ability or competence). He says, "you will only overcome this mountain, by my Spirit". WHAT SPIRIT IS THIS?

When the victory is won, it says the victory chant shall be 'grace, grace, grace did it!' The Spirit that guarantees the victory is the Spirit of Grace. GRACE IS THE KEY!

WHAT IS THIS GRACE? Unmerited favour. God's Riches At Christ's Expense. My definition is 'Divine enablement to do what you could not before'. Now, I am editing that definition a bit to 'Divine *Receivement*' [forgive the English]

Grace accessed by faith is the key to overcoming your mountain. Before you reach for might or power, reach for grace!

Key Thought: Grace is key to your victory.
Intelligent Prayer Point: Command the mountain, before you to move, by the grace of God.
Support Scriptures: John 1:16, Ephesians 2:8,9, Hebrews 4:16 & Titus 2:11-14

October 24

HEAR AND DO

Pilot Text: "But be ye doers of the word, and not hearers only, deceiving your own selves." – James 1:22

Deception is the major tool of the enemy against us. But, of the various types of deception the worst kind is self-deception. It is one thing for someone to try to deceive you, but it is totally another thing for you to deceive yourself.

According to James, the person who hears the word but does not do it, is deceiving himself. If all I do is hear the Word and never put it into practice, I am deceiving myself. So, how do you deceive yourself? You deceive yourself when you think that just hearing the Word is the blessing and then some weeks down the road, nothing has changed in your life, you start to conclude that the Word does not work - you are deceived. Why? Because it is the doer of the Word that is blessed in his deed (James 1:25). The real blessing is reserved for the doer.

I love where the Word of God is being shared with great insight, revelation and anointing. But now, I realize that I must take that word out of the realm of just hearing into the realm of doing. We feel blessed when we hear a strong prophetic Word, we get excited, light bulbs go off inside us, but the real blessing is in doing something with that word.

The Word does work. It works for the doer of the Word. To avoid the wrong conclusions and self-deception you have to HEAR AND DO.

Commit today to, not just hearing, but also to doing the Word. You need to do both: hear and do.
But some have stopped hearing, saying, "I haven't done anything with what I heard last". Don't get it twisted. You must continue to hear, because faith comes, not by having heard, but by hearing and continuing to hear. Just don't stop at only hearing, get out there and do it. Like *Nike* says, 'JUST DO IT!'

Key Thought: It is not enough to hear, you must also do the Word.
Intelligent Prayer Point: Pray for the grace to, not just hear, but to also do the Word.
Support Scriptures: Isaiah 55:11, Luke 11:28 & 2 Timothy 3:15-17

October 25

HEAVEN FIRST

Pilot Text: "…When you pray, say: Our Father in heaven, Hallowed be Your name. Your kingdom come, Your will be done on earth as it is in heaven." – Luke 11:2

Whatever a man is able to do, competently, in the public is a result of what he has done consistently in private. **Your outward competence is determined by your inward consecration.** The secret to Jesus' powerful public life was His private prayer life. Jesus' disciples realized that the secret to Jesus' powerful public life was His private prayer life. Realizing this, led them to ask Jesus to teach them to pray.

In teaching them to pray, Jesus taught them that, after the essential spiritual protocol of revered worship and praise of your heavenly father, your first priority should be His kingdom and His will on earth as it is in heaven.

In the kindergarten of prayers, we were taught that prayer was primarily a way to get what we want for ourselves, but here Jesus starts to teach us that Heaven's will and kingdom should be our primary objective in prayer.

Prayer is legal access for heaven on earth. Prayer is not so much a ladder from earth to heaven, but more a ladder for heaven to come to the earth. We are to pray for heaven first.

Matthew 6:33 says, "But seek ye first the kingdom of God, and his righteousness; and all these things shall be added unto you." PUT HEAVEN FIRST AND ALL OTHER THINGS WILL BE ADDED UNTO YOU.

Our prayer should constantly be 'let heaven come on earth'. Today, pray Heaven First. Pray Heaven on Earth!

Key Thought: Put heaven first and all other things will follow.
Intelligent Prayer Point: Insist heaven prevail over your life.
Support Scriptures: Proverbs 16:3, Matthew 6:9,10 & Matthew 18:18-20

October 26

HEED THE CALL

Pilot Text: "For the gifts and the calling of God are irrevocable." – Romans 11:29

There is a calling on your life. Paul prayed that we might know the hope of your calling. A calling speaks of a better tomorrow. A calling creates hope. That you were born, is evidence, enough, that you are called. Before you were formed in the womb you were known and before you came forth, your appointment was set (Jeremiah 1:5). A need precedes and necessitates the creation of a thing. A need existed that necessitated your arrival on the scene.

Your calling is written into your DNA. It doesn't let you sleep and wakes you up in the morning. It just won't leave you. With all the contradictions in your life, you still have a sense of 'there is more'. You are right. There is more. There is more to you than meets the eye. There is a calling on your life. The gifts and calling are irrevocable. Once given, they remain. What we do with them is, now, our responsibility.

What are your gifts? They point to your calling. What are your passions? They will inform your purpose. What need triggers your drive? That is a guide to your assignment. What are your natural competencies? They instruct your mission. What do your witnesses say of you? They confirm your direction.

Your Calling is your destination, your assignment and your purpose. Your Gifts/Talents are your inherent abilities. Your Skills are your acquired competences. You will need to master all these to excel in destiny. Acquiring skill is vital to advance, but better acquire skills that enhance your gifts and talents, rather than skills that have no relation to your calling.

Your gifts can give you clues to your purpose, but it is your calling that should inform how you use your gifts, talents and skills. It is time to heed the calling on your life, with all that you have.

Key Thought: There is a calling on your life.
Intelligent Prayer Point: Pray for the grace to take heed to your calling.
Support Scriptures: 1 Corinthians 1:26-29, 7:19,20, Ephesians 1:16-18 & 2 Timothy 1:8,9

October 27

HOLY IMPATIENCE

Pilot Text: "…imitate those who through faith and patience inherit the promises." – Hebrews 6:12

I have holy impatience. I don't know about you. I live with it everyday, sleep and wake up with it. Holy Impatience is an oxymoron. How can impatience be holy, or holy be impatient and is it a right state to be in? There are things that I expected to have already happened. There is where I expected to already be. There are many things that I expected would have been done yesterday. So, as regards these things, I am impatient. I want them done yesterday.

This is my impatience. I am impatient to see the will of God done in my life and the world. I am impatient to take delivery of my destiny. I am impatient to see growth in everything I do. I am impatient to see you maximizing all you've been given and being all that you can be. I am impatient to see the glory of God fill the earth as the waters cover the sea. I am holy impatient.

So, what is holy about my impatience? First is that, the object of my impatience is for the will of God to be done. Secondly, my impatience is tempered by a holy resolve to wait for God's timing. So, all the days of my appointed time will I wait till my change comes.

So, I must live with this impatience because it fuels my hunger to seek and my passion to pray. If I were not impatient, I might sleep while opportunities pass me by. But at the same time, I must hold this impatience in restraint by a holy resolve to wait for God, lest it drives me to compromise and sin.

So, every believer has to live with the reality of holy impatience in his bosom; for it is the pathway through which the promises are delivered. Are you holy impatient today?

Key Thought: Impatience is not always bad, sometimes, it is evidence of true desire for the things of God.
Intelligent Prayer Point: Ask God to use your holy impatience to bring you into a rich and abundant life in Him.
Support Scriptures: Philippians 3:12-15, 2 Timothy 1:6 & Hebrews 10:23-25

October 28

RUN WITH IT

Pilot Text: "I will stand upon my watch, and set me upon the tower, and will watch to see what he will say unto me, and what I shall answer when I am reproved. And the Lord answered me, and said, Write the vision, and make it plain upon tables, that he may run that readeth it" – Habakkuk 2:1-3.

Vision is vital; it is powerful and focuses energy for maximum results. Where there is no vision the people cast of restraint. Chaos reigns where there is no vision. Where there is no vision, the people perish (Proverbs 29:18) and as some have said: where there are no people, the vision will perish. But, I beg to differ: where there is no people, the vision is delayed and simply waits for a people that will pick it up again to run with it. The vision never perishes.

A vision is not meant to simply be a beautiful edifice to behold. We are meant to run with the vision. Vision is only actualized in the running with it; If you are not going to run with it, then you did not need it. To run, is to increase speed. Divine speed is one of the things we all want as believers, but speed is only relevant to the person who is going somewhere; to the person who is doing something, to the person who is running.

Speed is for he who runs. He who runs with Speed needs a clear Vision to run with. A clear Vision comes from God. God is eager to give you vision and the speed to run with it. The vision and speed come from God, but the running is your responsibility.

IT IS TIME TO RUN WITH IT!

Key Thought: The vision is meant for running. Run with it.
Intelligent Prayer Point: Pray for strength to run with the vision God has given you.
Support Scriptures: Proverbs 29:18 & 1 Corinthians 9:24-27

October 29

WHAT DO YOU DESIRE?

Pilot Text: "Therefore I say unto you, what things soever ye desire, when ye pray, believe that ye receive them, and ye shall have them"– Mark 11:24.

Desire is more important than we know; it is the drive behind sustained action. For desire, men will go to extreme lengths; without desire, drive can hardly be sustained. This is also true in prayer; desire drives prayer. Without desire prayer is often passionless and boring.

Desire is defined as "a strong feeling of wanting to have something or wishing for something to happen." If desire is so essential for sustained prayer, we must learn how it works and how to harness it. The starting place of effective prayer is not in the requests, but the desire. So, before I make the requests I should go to the place of desire. What do I desire? What do you desire? Where did that desire come from? I have to learn to cultivate right desires.

This is what the ministry of the word is meant to do. The ministry of the word is meant to give us visions of what is possible. It is meant to give us pictures of a preferred future. It is meant to create desire within us. Consistent exposure to the ministry of the word will create desire. That desire is, then, used to drive effective prayer. I take his word, which I desire, back to Him saying, "let your word and will be done".

What are you doing with your desires? Are you using your desires? What is informing your desires? the word of God or the words of men? "Whatever you desire, when you pray, believe the you receive them and you will have them." The process therefore is: desire – pray – believe – receive – have.

Key Thought: Desire is the womb of production.
Intelligent Prayer Point: Pray for the grace to cultivate a fervent desire for the right things; the will of God.
Support Scriptures: Matthew 21:22, James 5:16-17 & 1 Peter 2:2

October 30

THE ANATOMY OF DESIRE

Pilot Text: "...whatsoever you desire..." – Mark 11:24

That looks like a blank cheque; but is it? If I desire it, I can have it. Is it that simple? But, what if what I desire is wrong? What if what I desire is not God's will for me? It is not as simple as just desire it and you will have it. But Psalms 37:4 says "delight yourself in the Lord and he will give you the desires of your heart". He will give me what I desire. On the surface this looks like a blank cheque too; but is it?

What if he was not saying that he would give you what you desire, but that He would give you the very desire itself? He is not giving you what you desire, but rather, what TO desire. So, it was not about giving you the thing you desire, but really first, about giving you the desire for the right thing.

It looked like the only condition to getting whatever you desire was to delight yourself in the Lord. But to delight yourself in the Lord, is to be pliable as clay in His hands. So, it is not a blank cheque; in that whatever you desire, you will get but rather, if you allow God, He will work the right desires into you and that, you will get.

"For it is God who works in you both to will (desire) and to do for His good pleasure"– Philippians 2:13. If you allow God, He will work the right desires into you, so that your prayers will be according to His will and you would be confident of answers to your prayers (1 John 5:14).

"If you abide in me, and My words abide in you, you will ask what you desire, and it shall be done for you" – John 15:7. Do you see it? If you abide in Him and His Words abide in you; your desire will be granted because it would be His desire. When you abide, you become one with Him. So, I am pressing into His presence in worship and prayer for Him to give me the Desires of my heart. Do you understand?

Key Thought: If you allow God, He will work the right desires into you.
Intelligent Prayer Point: Pray that the Holy spirit will birth the desire for the right things within you.
Support Scriptures: John 15:7, Romans 8:5,6 & Colossians 3:1,2

October 31

WORKING IT IN YOU

Pilot Text: "For it is God who works in you both to will (Desire) and to do of His good pleasure (Will)" – Philippians 2:13

God has so much that he wants to give and wants to do in your life. His thoughts for you are not of evil but of peace to give you a future and a hope (Jeremiah 29:11). "...Eye has not seen, nor ear heard, nor have entered into the heart of man the things which God has prepared for those who love Him" – 1 Corinthians 2:9.

God has awesome untold things in store for you. But, there is a pathway He has to work through, to get it across to you. He has to work it into your desire, then you take that desire into the place of prayer and ask for it, believe that you receive it and you will have it (Mark 11:24).

Key therefore, is your allowing God to work the right desires into you. You have to be pliable in His hands, letting Him mold you. Let His words create the right desires in you, regardless of how impossible it might seem. But, there is something greatly encouraging about God-given desire. God-given desire is proof that what you desire already exists, even if not yet in the natural; it exists in the heart of God, for you.

My desire for a car tells me that the car exists already. My desire for a house indicates that the house already exists. My desire for a spouse means a spouse is being prepared somewhere for me. My desire for financial liberty proves that it is possible.

So now, I can rejoice in the desire because it is the proof that what I desire exists and it is just a matter of my faithfully following God's process and the patience of time, for me to get it. It is just a matter of time; it is on the way. Do you believe it?

Key Thought: God is working great and wonderful things into your heart, if you allow Him.
Intelligent Prayer Point: Pray for God to mold your desires into His desires.
Support Scriptures: Psalm 31:19, Isaiah 64:14 & James 1:12

November 1

IT IS IN THE SEED

Pilot Text: "... it is like a grain of mustard seed, when sown it is in the earth, is less than all the seeds on earth: but when it is sown, it grows up and becomes greater than all..." – Mark 4:30-32

It may start small, but it will become great. The great tree starts out as a tiny seed. Everything starts as a seed; never despise a seed because you do not know what that seed will become. Don't look down on the seed.

A seed speaks of potential. Potential is not what you have already done but what you could do. "But a seed is a seed", someone says. A seed is not just a seed. Locked in a seed are untold potential and infinite possibilities. God always starts with a seed. God starts small, so, never despise small beginnings. Scripture says "though your beginning was small, yet your latter end will greatly increase" – Job 8:7. "Oh, that they were wise, that they understood this, that they would consider their latter end" – Deuteronomy 32:29.

When you plant the Chinese bamboo seed, it quickly sprouts from the ground, then stays the same for four long years. Then, in the fifth year, it grows three feet per day, till it reaches 90 feet tall; that is exponential growth! Sometimes, your life can be like the Chinese bamboo tree, your growth is coming; so, protect your seed.

What is your seed? Your seed is your potential. Your seed is your product; it is your jar of oil. Your seed is your gift; it is your five fish and two loaves. Your seed is your competence; it is your five stones and sling shot. Your seed is your skill; it is the staff in your hand. Your seed is your talent; it is your influence.

But before you can unlock the potential in your seed, it must go through a process. Today, re-evaluate the value of your seed.
Tomorrow, we will commence discussing the process of the seed.

Key Thought: Locked in a seed are untold potential and infinite possibilities
Intelligent Prayer Point: Pray that God will open your eyes to see the seed that He has put in your hands.
Support Scriptures: Exodus 4:2, Zechariah 4:10 & Matthew 13:32,33

November 2

THE SEED MUST BE SOWN

Pilot Text: '...a mustard seed... when it is sown, it grows up and becomes greater...' – Mark 4:31-32

Before the seed can unlock its potential within, it must go through a process. We want the outcome, but don't want the input. We want the victory, but don't want the battle. We want the glory, but don't want the story. We want the greatness, but don't want the process. Before a seed can become great, it has to go through a process: this is the process of the seed.

The first step in the process of the seed is that it must be sown; sow it. The seed will never release what it has within unless it is first sown. If you keep your seed, that is all you will have, just a seed. Your seed represents your life. If you try to keep your seed, you will ultimately lose it. You can only preserve and perpetuate the life of your seed by sowing it.

"For whoever desires to save his life will lose it, but whoever loses his life for My sake will find it" – Matthew 16:25. It is in giving your life, freely, for the Kingdom's sake, that you actually find it; you have to sow your seed.

To be sown is to be buried in the earth: to be buried under some dirt, under some mess. So, they took Jesus and buried Him in the earth, under some mess, but did not realize that they were actually sowing Him as seed; unless a seed is sown it abides alone. When Jesus came back from the grave, He did not come back alone like a seed sown; he came back multiplied in you and me.

You have to be sown in the earth before what is within you can be unleashed. Out of the mess is coming a message. Lose yourself in God to find your real self.

Don't eat your seed, don't keep your seed; sow your seed today.

Key Thought: Your seed represents your life; you can only preserve and perpetuate the life of your seed by sowing it.
Intelligent Prayer Point: Pray that your life will become a living sacrifice to God, submitting wholly to be used for his good pleasure.
Support Scriptures: John 12:24, Romans 14:9 & 1 Corinthians 15:36

November 3

THE SEED MUST DIE

Pilot Text: "Most assuredly, I say to you, unless a grain of wheat falls into the ground and dies, it remains alone..." – John 12:24

The second step in the process of the seed is that it must die. When you have sown your seed, you must resist the temptation to go dig it up to check whether it is growing. You must let it die. You must die to your seed and your seed must die to you.

To die is to be separated from this world. Your seed must die to the world that it knew: buried in the earth, separated. You have got to sow your seed and walk away in faith. You sow your financial seed and walk away with your eyes set on God, Who is the One that brings the increase.

If you take it upon yourself to become a monitoring spirit, checking for every detail of how your financial seed is utilized in the kingdom, then it was not a sown seed, it is not dead to you and you are not dead to it. If that is the case, it is, at best, only a seed and cannot yield the untold potential in it. Before your seed can bring returns, you have to die to your seed and your seed has to die to you.

Mark 4:26,27 says the sower sleeps by night and rises by day after sowing his seed and knows not how the seed grows. There is a "know not how" dimension to seed sowing. If you insist on knowing every detail of the process, you will abort it. The "know not how" dimension is the faith dimension. Die to your seed and let your seed die to you. Don't dig up your seed but water it, water it with the right words of confessions.

Key Thought: Before your seed can bring returns, you have to die to your seed and your seed has to die to you.
Intelligent Prayer Point: Declare today, "I am coming back, I will rise again, I will live again, my seed will return".
Support Scriptures: Psalms 126:6, 1 Corinthians 15:36-38 & Romans 14:9

November 4

BREAK THROUGH THE EARTH

Pilot Text: "...a man sows seed... the seed should sprout and grow" – Mark 4:26-27.

The third step in the process of the seed is that the seed must break through the earth. The seed has been sown. You have died to it and it has died to you. Now, it must break through the earth.

The seed has to push through the earth towards the call of the sun. You have to push through that mess towards the call of the Son of Righteousness. The seed has to break through the earth; it has to press back the muck and come out. You and your gift have to push through the ridicule and scorn; you have to survive the slander and backbiting; you have to breakthrough the dirt of your past; you have to press back the muck of contradictions and complexities.

The seed has to do this by itself; you cannot help the seed to this. If you try to help the seed to this by digging it up or creating an easy pathway for it, it will not survive afterwards. The chick must break out of the shell by itself, if it will survive in the new world. The strength it takes to break out of the shell is the same strength it will take to survive in the new world. You have to break through the earth yourself!

The pressure is not meant to kill you, but rather, to strengthen you. The pain is for gain. The test is for a testimony. The trial is for a triumph. What doesn't kill you only makes you stronger. What killed you (because the seed must die) rebirths you anew.

Whatever you are going through right now, is only making you stronger and rebirthing you anew! Tough times don't last, but tough people do.

Key Thought: It is time to break through the earth.
Intelligent Prayer Point: Pray that you now breakthrough whatever represents the hard ground in your life.
Support Scriptures: Ecclesiastes 11:6, Hosea 10:12 & Luke 12:54

November 5

FIRST THE BLADE

Pilot Text: "For the earth yields crops by itself: "first the blade", then the head, after that the full grain in the head" – Mark 4:28.

Step four in the process of the seed is "first the blade." The blade is the small leaf-like sprout that you see emerging out of the earth; it is tiny and almost insignificant. If you are not observant, you could miss it. It is the first sign that what was dead is coming back to life.

The lesson here, is that you have to learn to rejoice at little signs. The blade represents little signs. Little signs point to big destinations (the sign is always smaller than what it is pointing to). Little signs precede big things; rejoice at little signs.

Dance in faith at the first sign of a turning because if the blade could make it out, the whole plant is coming out too. If your hand could make it out, your body is following soon after. If your sister could testify, know its just a matter of time, you'll be up next. If somehow, you paid the gas bill, you'll make the mortgage payment too. If you killed the bear, the lion is going down. If you defeated the lion, then tell me, "who is Goliath?"

All Elijah saw was a cloud the size of a man's hand and he told Ahad to hurry to the city that the rain stop him not. Rejoice at little signs, because the great follows after. Look out for little signs today and rejoice when you see them, because something is about to happen.

Key Thought: Rejoice at little signs, they precede the big things.
Intelligent Prayer Point: Pray that your eyes are open to recognise the little signs.
Support Scriptures: 1 Kings 18:44, Zechariah 4:10 & Luke 21:28

November 6

THEN THE HEAD

Pilot Text: "For the earth yields crops by itself: first the blade, then the head, after that the full grain in the head." – Mark 4:28

The fifth step in the process of the seed is "then the head". In the corn plant, the head is the leafy container that will house the corn that will follow; this speaks of preparation. Now that I have seen the blade, I must prepare for what is following.

Elijah saw the cloud the size of man's fist and told Ahad to race ahead to the city lest the rain stop him. Now that you have a jar of oil, go borrow many more vessels because the oil is about to flow. Dig ditches all through this valley, though you see no wind nor rain yet this valley will be filled with water (2 Kings 3:16,17)

Get ready, get ready, get ready; something is about to happen! Prepare for what is about to come; get your structure in place. Get your systems in place. Get your relationships in order; something is about to happen.

The head is the container for the corn. The size of your container will determine the size of corn you can receive. Your head is the seat of your mind and soul. Expand your thinking to accommodate what God is about to do. As a man thinks, so he is. If you are coming out, you are coming out, head first. Embrace the mind of Christ (a mind of infinite possibilities) to receive what Christ gives.

Get ready, get ready, get ready… something is about to happen.

Key Thought: Now that I have seen the blade, I must prepare for what is following.
Intelligent Prayer Point: Pray for understanding to know how to prepare for the breakthrough that is coming.
Support Scriptures: Isaiah 30:23, Isaiah 55:10 & Hosea 2:21

November 7

THE FULL GRAIN IN THE HEAD

Pilot Text: "For the earth yields crops by itself: first the blade, then the head, after that the full grain in the head" – Mark 4:28.

The sixth step in the process of the seed is "then the full grain in the head". The "head" is the structure you create for the harvest to follow. The harvest will fill the structure you create for it. So, your structure will either limit or liberate your harvest.

However, at this stage, the harvest is still hidden in the "head": at this stage, your structure hides your progress and conceals your success. The grain is not yet seen because it is hidden in the head of corn; this is hidden growth. There is a portion of your growth that must be in secret: that must be hidden growth. Hidden from preying eyes. Hidden in the structure. Hidden in the systems. Hidden in service.

You are hidden on purpose, for a purpose. You are hidden from premature exposure. You are hidden from unripe ingestion. You are hidden so you don't falter on the main stage. You are hidden so that the enemy cannot pluck out your grain before it is mature. You are hidden so that your opponents won't see you coming.

This is why, when you shine on the main stage, they say "he was an overnight success" or "where did he come from"; because they did not see your hidden growth. They won't see you coming. Most significant growth take place in the night while you were sleeping; learn to grow in the dark.

Rejoice at hidden growth because it is for your good. It is all working together for your good.

Key Thought: The structure you create will either limit or liberate your harvest.
Intelligent Prayer Point: Pray for wisdom to build the right structures in preparation for your harvest.
Support Scriptures: Psalm 65:12, Isaiah 61:11 & Micah 4:4

November 8

WHAT DO YOU CALL IT?

Pilot Text: "And out of the ground the Lord God formed every beast of the field, and every fowl of the air; and brought them unto Adam to see what he would call them: and whatsoever Adam called every living creature, that was the name thereof" – Genesis 2:19

Names and naming is so important that it was the next most important assignment after giving Adam the assignment of tending and keeping the garden. God brought all the animals to Adam to see what He would call them. This was a responsibility given to Adam and God did not interfere. God wanted to see what Adam would call them, and whatever he called them, was their name from then on. Another translation says: "as he called them, so they were."

Can you imagine the multiplied thousands of animals that Adam had to name? Why did God put Adam through this repetitive process? I believe God was teaching Adam that life and death are in the power of the tongue (Proverbs 18:21). God was involving Adam in the creative process; whatever he called them, is what they were or became. He wanted Adam to realize that your world is created by your words: by what you name it.

It doesn't really take on a nature till you name it. Your world is not determined by what you see but by what you call it: what you name it. What are you naming your world today? Is it an end or just a bend? What do you call it? Is it a refusal or a redirection; What do you call it? It's not a dumping; it is a pumping to the next level. It's not an exit it's an entry into something new. Stop mourning the exit and start celebrating the entry. It is determined by what you call it. It is not an end; it is a new beginning.

Today, recreate your World with your words. What are you calling it?

Key Thought: Your world is created by your words: by what you name it.
Intelligent Prayer Point: Pray that the Holy Spirit will inspire you to speak the words you need to frame your world.
Support Scriptures: Proverbs 13:2-3, Isaiah 3:10 & Matthew 12:37

November 9

WHAT IS A NAME?

Pilot Text: "I will make your name great..." – Genesis 12:2.

How do we define a name? A name is a word or set of words by which a person, animal, place or thing is known, addressed, or referred to.

A name is a means of identification; it is the definition of a thing and a point of reference. It is also a mark of differentiation and becomes the total embodiment of a person: representative of the person.

A name becomes an association. So, when I hear a name, I make an association. For example, what comes to mind when you hear the names, Lewis Hamilton, Jessica Ennis, Tiger Woods, David Cameron, Michael Jordon, Theo Walcott, Andy Murray...? When people hear your name what do they associate you with: efficiency or excuses? Ouch!

What do we mean, when we say "he made a name for himself?" We mean a strong association has been made with his name, so that when his name is mentioned, most people think of the same thing. For example Bill Gates, Steve Jobs, Barack Obama, and Malala Yousafzai: these ones have made names for themselves.

The only challenge with making a name for yourself is that you have to sustain it yourself. When other men make a name great; that man-made-man will also be a man-pulled-down-man. But, there is another category of men with great names, who are descendants of Abraham, whose name God made great. When God makes your name great, there is nothing anyone can do about it (try though they might).

A name is also a signature, particularly in the day we live in. We are fast moving from physical signatures to virtual and digital signatures: where your name will be your signature. So, my question today is: what is your name?

Key Thought: Whatever you call it; is what it is or will become.
Intelligent Prayer Point: Pray that you will always have the "God inspired name" you need for every circumstance.
Support Scriptures: Psalms 91:41, Proverbs 10:7, 22:11 & Philippians 2:9

November 10

A GOOD NAME

Pilot Text: "A good name is to be chosen rather than great riches, loving favor rather than silver and gold" – Proverbs 22:1

A name is not just a means of identification & differentiation, but it also points to our ancestry, our lineage and heritage. In asking for your surname, I am asking for your ancestry. There are doors that only a good name can open; not even riches can force them open. There are places that you simply cannot access without the right name.

As a parent, one thing that you must strive to bequeath to your children (even if you fail to give them silver or gold), is to give them a good name. There are places a good name will take them that silver and gold will not (best to give them both, of course).

Knowing the value of a good name, often when sending our children off to college, we charge them not to soil our good name. Our concern is the fact that the child might not know the value of the name, having not had to do anything to earn it: he was just born into it.

Peter and John said "silver and gold we have not but what we have we give you. In the name of Jesus Christ of Nazareth rise up and walk." Like a child born into a good home, we have been given a name we did not earn, buy or lobby for. We were simply born into it when we accepted Jesus. Now, at that name, every knee must bow and every tongue confess. That name is above every other name. Through that name, you and I have access to stupendous help and assistance.

You must learn to value and use the awesome name of Jesus that you have been given; it is a good name. What door have you been trying to access? Maybe you have been using the wrong name. Today, thank God for the good name of Jesus and use it in faith.

Key Thought: You must learn to value and use the awesome name of Jesus that you have been given; it is a good name
Intelligent Prayer Point: Thank God for name of Jesus and begin to pronounce that name over every long standing challenge you are facing right now, commanding it to bow.
Support Scriptures: Matthew 28:18, John 17:12 & Ephesians 1:20,21

November 11

WHAT IS HIS AND YOUR NAME?

Pilot Text: "Who do men say that I the Son of Man am? And they said, some say John the Baptist, some Elijah, and others Jeremiah or one of the prophets. He said to them, But who do you say that I am" – Matt. 16:13-15.

They were quick to offer the opinion of others, but when asked their own opinion, their silence was deafening. Then, Simon stepped up to the plate and said: "you are the Christ." There are those who are concerned with what people say. They know the various schools of thought. Their lives are governed by other people's opinions: they are consumed with what people will say, think or do; swinging between opinions without taking a personal authentic position. The truth is there are scarce few in our lives whose opinions of us should really matter.

After wading through the pool of public opinion, Jesus asked, "who do you say that I am". "What do you say?" That is what really matters. What you say is what will most affect your life and destiny. He is also teaching that it is not self-determination that comes first, but rather, God-finding: it is not about your name first, but about His. In order to find yourself you must first find God.

Simon found God and called Him by name. Christ turned around and said: "you will no longer be Simon, but now Peter". Simon meant reed; but Peter means stone. This was a movement from instability to stability, premised on a revelation of God.

When Simon found God, he got a name change. When you find God, your name will change. When you find God you find the real you: your name changes. As you seek God out today, I feel a name change coming on. He is going to change your name from victim to victor, from sick to healed, from poor to rich; but first, what is His name to you?

Key Thought: When you find God, you find the real you and your name changes.
Intelligent Prayer Point: Pray for a deeper revelation of the power in the name of Christ.
Support Scriptures: Jeremiah 1:5, Mark 8:27-29 & 2 Corinthians 2:9-10

November 12

SO WHAT IS YOUR NAME?

Pilot Text: "I will not let you go unless you bless me" – Genesis 32:26

This was Jacob's cry after a night of wrestling with God. Let us learn from Jacob's pathway to blessing. Jacob realized that he had to confront his past, in order to engage his future. He had to return home; the prodigal must return.

On the journey home, he sent his family and stuff ahead; he separated himself from things till he was left alone. There are certain levels you will not attain till you are left alone. Every once in a while you need to stop the noise, remove the distractions and get alone with God.

It is when you are left alone that you confront the real you; when you remove all those props that you use to accessorize and define yourself and come face to face with the real you. Jacob wrestled with an angel till the break of day. You have to willing to wrestle some things to the ground. Wrestle till your limp is revealed. Wrestle till the weakness you need to address is apparent. Wrestle to the point of desperation. God answers desperate people – "I will not let you go unless You bless me".

The angel asked "what is your name?" He was saying, "I cannot bless you until I know your name". God does not anoint masks; what is your name? When all the props are gone, when the make-up is washed off, when the fronts are lifted, when the act is over and the pretense stopps; what is your name? Outside what you do, what you have achieved, your position, status, what you drive, wear or live in: what is your name?

Jacob answered: "I am Jacob." Jacob means supplanter, con artist, deceiver; He had to admit his failings in order to get blessed. You have to be willing to come clean and admit that you are Jacob. You cannot be Israel till you first admit that you are Jacob. What is your name?

Key Thought: Every once in a while, you need to stop the noise, remove the distractions and get alone with God.
Intelligent Prayer Point: Pray for a revelation of the name God has given you.
Support Scriptures: I Chronicles 4:10, Isaiah 41:9, 43:1, 45:4 & Hosea 12:4

November 13

JACOB OR ISRAEL

Pilot Text: "So He said to him, what is your name? He said, Jacob. And He said, your name shall no longer be called Jacob, but Israel" – Genesis 32:27,28.

Jacob means heel grabber, supplanter, con artist or even deceiver. Israel means prince of God. Before Jacob was made Israel, He had to first admit that he was Jacob. I know this goes against the grain and it is a struggle to admit it, but admit you must: I am Jacob.

I am prideful, I am resentful, I am judgmental, I am bitter, I am a liar, I am a thief. I know it tastes bitter in the mouth as you admit it, but this is the pathway. I am afraid, I am a fornicator, I am an adulterer, I am insecure, I am full of doubt, I am arrogant, I am condescending, I am Jacob.

It was only when Jacob was willing to admit that he was Jacob that God could bless him. It was only after he admitted who he was that God could make him who he is. It was only after he admitted who he was that God gave him a name change.

I am a word of faith and new creation realities teacher; but I believe this vital step of admission is often skipped hence, we are losing the real power of a divine name change. There has to be an admission of our inadequacy before God comes in with His adequacy. According to scripture: "His strength is made perfect in my weakness"– 2 Corinthians 12:9.

When you meet God with no masks or pretenses, then, He changes your name. Jacob becomes Israel, Abram becomes Abraham, Sarai becomes Sarah, Simon becomes Peter and Saul becomes Paul. I feel a name change coming on: your name is about to change. No longer con artist, now prince of God. No longer poor, now rich. No longer weak, now strong. No longer confused, but now directed. No longer sick, now healed. No longer cast down, now lifted up. No longer dismayed, now at peace.

So what is your name? I am no longer Jacob; I am Israel.

Key Thought: There has to be an admission of our inadequacy before God comes in with His adequacy.

Intelligent Prayer Point: Confess your need to God and your faith to the world, declaring your name change in the name of Jesus Christ.

Support Scriptures: Exodus 3:11-12, 1 Corinthians 2:3-5 & Ephesians 3:16

November 14

WHAT IS IN A NAME?

Pilot Text: 'A good name is to be chosen rather than great riches…' – Proverbs 22:1

An honorable father will admonish his son to protect his good name that he has painstakingly built over many years. A good father will not only leave his children wealth but also a good name. It's not all about the phonetics of a name. It is about what a name is associated with.

What associations come to mind when you hear certain names? Steve Jobs? Billy Graham? Myles Munroe? Bill Gates? Brian Tracy? Oprah Winfrey? T.D. Jakes? Mike Murdock?

When people hear your name, what associations come to their mind? Late? Not loyal? Excellent? Dependable? Self-centered? Selfless? Delivers? Unreliable? Optimist? Pessimist? Negative? Positive? Truthful? Liar? Builder? Leader? Detractor? Weak? Strong?

Your name is about your reputation. What name are you building for yourself? Everything you do is building your name (consciously or unconsciously)? Why not be deliberate about building your name today?

It even goes beyond the original meaning of a name. The name Jabez means 'bringer of sorrow'. This was the name given to him by his mother because of the pain she was in when he was born.

But when Jabez came of age, he asked the Lord to bless him indeed and enlarge his territory. God answered him and it is recorded that he was more honorable than his brothers (1 Chronicles 4:9,10). In effect, God changed his name such that when we hear the name Jabez today we don't think 'sorrow', we think 'he that has been blessed indeed'.

Saul was persecuting the Church but when he met the Lord he became Paul, the promoter of the Church. Simon became Peter. Jacob became Israel. God is still in the business of changing names. When you discover God, you will discover the new you.

Whether it is a literal change of name or a change in the associations made with your name, I sense a name change coming on. Do you believe it?

Key Thought: What associations come with your name? Be deliberate in building a good name.
Intelligent Prayer Point: Pray that God will take you deeper in the discovery of who He has made you to be.
Support Scriptures: Ecclesiastes 7:1, Isaiah 62:2 & 2 Corinthians 5:17

November 15

HE WILL RESTORE DOUBLE

Pilot Text: "Return to the stronghold, you prisoners of hope. Even today I declare that I will restore double to you." – Zechariah 9:12

Our God is a God of restoration. He will restore! But to be a candidate for restoration, you must have lost something. Restoration is irrelevant if nothing has been lost. So, what did you lose? What did we lose?

God made sure that man had everything that he needed in the beginning. He placed him in a garden of abundance: Eden. But, when man disobeyed God and sinned, he lost it all. So, from Genesis Chapter 3 to the end of the Bible, we see God's restoration plan.

Right from the beginning, God already had restoration on His mind. When man sinned and the glory departed, he saw that he was naked. God covered them with clothes of skin. Where did He get the clothes of skin? I believe God killed an animal in their stead and took the skin from the animal and clothed them with it. I believe that animal was a lamb. Revelations 13:7 says '…the Lamb slain from the foundation of the world.' I also believe this because '…all things are purified with blood, and without shedding of blood there is no remission.' – Hebrews 9:22. So, blood had to be shed for the remission of the sin of Adam and Eve. The lamb that was slain in the beginning was a typology of the Lamb of God that would be slain at Calvary. So, right from the beginning, we see God unveiling His restoration plan. By the sacrifice of the Lamb, you and I would be restored.

"He came that we may have life and have it more abundantly" John 10:10. He is saying 'Even today, I will restore double!' Get ready for restoration!

Key Thought: God is eager to wipe the slate clean of sin and fully restore all that has been lost.
Intelligent Prayer Point: Ask that the Lord's restoration power will saturate your life.
Support Scriptures: Zephaniah 3:17, John 8:35 & Acts 23:11

November 16

RESTORING BLOOD

Pilot Text: "to Jesus the Mediator of the new covenant, and to the blood of sprinkling that speaks better things than that of Abel." – Hebrews 12:24

Cain and Abel made offerings unto the Lord. Abel's sacrifice of a lamb was accepted while Cain's offering of the fruit of the ground was not. When Cain was upset, God said 'why are you angry? If you had done the right thing would you not have been accepted?' So, Cain knew what the right thing was and did not do it. Their parents, Adam & Eve had taught them, that the sacrifice that is acceptable to God for sins is the blood sacrifice.

Cain went on to kill Abel and God asked 'is it not the voice of your brother's blood that I hear crying from the ground…'
The first man to die on the face of the earth was murdered. The blood of Abel cried from the ground for vengeance and judgment. A cycle of sin and death was now fully in motion.

Fast forward to Jesus on the cross. After his death on the cross, to confirm that He was indeed dead, the soldiers pierced Him in his side with a spear and blood and water gushed out and His blood hit the same earth that Abel's blood had hit. But where Abel's blood cried for vengeance and judgment, Jesus' blood spoke forgiveness and redemption. He said "forgive them for they know not what they do". He broke the cycle of sin and death and set up the cycle of the spirit of life in Christ Jesus for anyone that believes. His blood touching the earth also reversed the curse on the earth. So now, you can demand that the earth must yield its increase unto you.

Praise God for His restoring blood. Take advantage of the speakings of the blood, today and speak restoration of everything that was lost.

Key Thought: There is power, power, wonder-working power in the blood of the Lamb.
Intelligent Prayer Point: Employ the speaking of the blood of Jesus and all that it represents against every plot of the enemy.
Support Scriptures: 1 Peter 1:18,19, 1 John 1:7 & Revelation 5:12

November 17

CANDIDATE FOR RESTORATION

Pilot Text: "Return to the stronghold, you prisoners of hope. Even today I declare that I will restore double to you." – Zechariah 9:12

Our God is a God of restoration. Our God is still in the business of restoration. The whole of the Bible is about restoration. Praise God for restoration.

But for restoration to take place, it means something was lost. So to be a candidate for restoration I must have lost something.

We want restoration, but we don't want loss. We want the testimony, but we don't want the test. We want the triumph, but we don't want the trial. Stop crying over your loss. It is your loss that has made you a candidate for restoration. Now, I rejoice and dance at my loss because I know it is a set up for my restoration.

And when God restores, He restores double for my trouble. Ask Job.

Other key characteristics of the candidates for restoration is that they are prisoners of hope and faith walkers. You have to keep hope alive and walk by faith, if you will experience the restoration of God.

He is going to restore double for your trouble. Change your mourning into dancing. Turn your crying into singing. Exchange your moaning for praising. The God of restoration is on His way!

Today, make a list of things you have lost and start believing for God's restoration.

Key Thought: Loss, hope and faith all make you a candidate for restoration.
Intelligent Prayer Point: Pray for total restoration in your life.
Support Scriptures: Exodus 12:13, Leviticus 17:11 & Luke 7:32

November 18

GOD'S RESTORATION

Pilot Text: "So I will restore to you the years that the swarming locust has eaten, the crawling locust, the consuming locust, and the chewing locust, My great army which I sent among you." – Joel 2:25

Our God is a God of restoration. God is committed to bringing restoration into the lives of His own. But when God restores, He does not restore like man attempts to restore. Man attempts to restore you to where he thinks you should be: at par with your colleagues. When God restores He takes you ahead of your colleagues.

God does not restore as it was or should have been but better than it ever was.
SO, DO NOT FIXATE ON HOW IT WAS, ON WHO IT WAS, because God will restore better than it was. So, John walked out on you and you've been fixating on God restoring John back into your life when God has Peter lined up for you and Peter is so much better than John, but because you are still fixated on John, you cannot see Peter.

Break the fixation! Stop putting God in a box. Let God restore anyway and anyhow He wants to restore. He might not give you back exactly who or what you lost, but one thing I can guarantee is that God will give you back better: He will exceed your expectations.

As much as man might try to restore, one thing man cannot restore is time. But God said He would restore the years. He is the master of time, space and the universe. He restores time. He does not reverse time, but He will make it such that the time lost will become irrelevant and better still, He will make the seeming loss of time work together for your good.

HE KNOWS HOW TO MAKE IT SWEETER LATER. BELIEVE FOR GOD'S RESTORATION TODAY!

Key Thought: God's restoration is not limited to just things, but also time.
Intelligent Prayer Point: Pray for the miraculous restoration of any and all time you might have lost.
Support Scriptures: Amos 9:11, Acts 3:21 & 1 Corinthians 15:58

November 19

KEY TO RESTORATION

Pilot Text: "Return to the stronghold, you prisoners of hope. Even today I declare that I will restore double to you." – Zechariah 9:12

The candidate for restoration of double in the text is designated a prisoner of hope. If you will have God's restoration, you have to be a prisoner of hope. Without hope you cannot attract God's restoration. You have to be a prisoner of hope. What a paradox of terms: a prisoner, yet hopeful.

Sometimes, hope can feel like a prison. I know that frustration of hope. "Hope deferred makes the heart sick." – Proverbs 13:12.

"(Abraham) who against hope believed in hope…" – Romans 4:18. Abraham, our father of faith was a prisoner of hope. You have to be hopelessly optimistic. Though the embrace of hope can be often uncomfortable and sometimes makes you look foolish, you cannot let go of hope. Even when you want to let go of hope, hope won't let you go. It is said that as long as there is life there is hope. I believe the converse is as true: As long as there is hope there is life (the suicidal have lost all hope). Don't let go of your hope.

Your hope gives focus to your faith. So, your hope and faith work together to attract God's restoration. "But without faith it is impossible to please Him, for he who comes to God must believe that He is, and that He is a rewarder (restorer)..." – Hebrews 11:6. Faith is essential for restoration.

God's restoration happens in an atmosphere of faith. There has to be hope and faith for restoration. Get ready for restoration. You have got to be expectant. Something good will happen for you today. God's restoration can happen at any time.

Turn the next corner expectant... Something is about to happen

Key Thought: Hope and faith are key to God's restoration.
Intelligent Prayer Point: Pray for the tenacity to hold on to your hope and faith.
Support Scriptures: 2 Kings 7:1, Proverbs 6:30,31 & John 8:35

November 20

GET READY FOR RESTORATION

Pilot Text: "You have sown much, and bring in little…And he who earns wages, earns wages to put into a bag with holes." – Haggai 1:6

So what if stupendous restoration were to happen to you today? What would you do with it? If you were given 100,000 pounds today, what would you do with it?

The proof that you are truly expecting something is that you make plans for it. If you are expecting God to bring restoration into your life, what plans do you have for the restoration when it arrives? Many lose their restoration almost as soon as it arrives because they had no plans on how to utilize and maximize the restoration. So, they put their restoration in the proverbial bag with holes. Are you really ready for restoration?

WILL GOD RESTORE IT, IF YOU ARE GOING TO LOSE IT AGAIN? Sometimes, what is delaying the restoration is that you have not developed the capacity to retain what He wants to restore to you. So, creating room for the restoration is more than just showing expectation or excitement or shouting at the prospect of restoration, it also involves real life expansions and addressing of issues.

So, you have to set structures in place to accommodate the restoration. You cannot grow beyond your structure. If your capacity can only hold 500mls, you will only hold 500mls, even if God gives you 10,000mls.

You also have to address the issue of HOW you lost it in the first place? HOW DID YOU LOSE IT IN THE FIRST PLACE? If you do not address that issue, you are going to lose it all over again. How did you lose the job, the money, the relationship, the whatever?

I see restoration on the horizon, but are you ready for it? GET READY FOR RESTORATION.

Key Thought: Your faith preparation for restoration is key to the restoration.
Intelligent Prayer Point: Decree that God is restoring back to you multiplied all that the devil stole from you.
Support Scriptures: Psalms 51:12, Jeremiah 30:17 & Joel 2:25

November 21

SEVENFOLD RESTORATION… IF THE THIEF BE CAUGHT

Pilot Text: "If the thief be caught, he must restore sevenfold…" – Proverbs 6:31

There are various levels of restoration. Our God is the God of restoration. He will restore double. He will restore sevenfold!

But in our text, there is conditionality. IF THE THIEF BE CAUGHT! The sevenfold restoration is dependent on the thief being caught. You have to catch the thief.

This still speaks of addressing the issues in your past that led to the loss in the first place. It speaks of setting a trap to catch the thieves in your past that have stolen so much from you. Identify them and catch them. Thieves such as laziness, defensiveness, selfishness, anger, impatience, fear, doubt, inferiority complex, pride and so many others. THE THIEF MUST BE CAUGHT! Catch the thief or he is going to make away with your stuff scot-free. Catch the thief and he has to restore sevenfold whatever he stole.

But, I've got good news for you; the chief thief has already been caught. Jesus 'disarmed principalities and powers, He made a public spectacle of them, triumphing over them in it (the cross)." Colossians 2:15. Jesus has caught and disarmed the chief thief. Hallelujah! The thief has been caught.

So, that means I now have the right to demand a sevenfold restoration of all that the devil stole. You have to take authority over the enemy because he would still attempt to hold unto what is no longer his. There will be no restoration without spiritual warfare. You have to engage the enemy and take back everything he stole.

IT IS TIME FOR YOUR SEVENFOLD RESTORATION!

Key Thought: Once the thief is caught, sevenfold restoration is your right.
Intelligent Prayer Point: Pray that you would be able to identify and catch every thief in your life and that sevenfold restoration would be yours.
Support Scriptures: Psalms 23:3, Psalms 39:14 & Proverbs 6:31

November 22

RE-STORE

Pilot Text: 'So I will restore to you the years…' – Joel 2:25

Jesus came to fill the gaps. Filling the gaps is restoring what was lost. Jesus came with a restoration mandate. He came to restore that which was lost.

We have learnt a lot on restoration, so far.
Restoration is the combination of two words – 'Rest' and 'Oration'
For Restoration to happen you have to operate from a position of resting on the finished work of Christ and orating the promises of God. Orate yourself into Rest-oration.

But God just gave me a fresh insight.
Restore is the combination of two words also – 'RE' and 'STORE'. The 'RE' is for REturn. God said to me that for Him to REturn all that He wants to return into your life, you have to have a Store for Him to restore into.

What is a store or storehouse? A store is a place where things are kept for future use or sale. A storehouse is a building used for storing goods.

So what does it mean to have a store or storehouse for God to restore into? A store or storehouse speaks of a structure for controlling supply and demand and projecting into tomorrow.

So what are you going to do with the restoration? What structures or systems have you put in place to maximize God's restoration in your life? What if it is the lack of a store that is delaying the restoration that God has in mind for you? It takes faith to build a store when you don't seem to have anything yet. But will you build today? God wants to restore, but do you have a store in place to receive it?

Key Thought: Get your stores in order because restoration is on the horizon.
Intelligent Prayer Point: Ask that the Holy Spirit position you rightly, for God's restoration, so that you will, without fail, recover all.
Support Scriptures: 1 Samuel 30:8, Isaiah 54:2, Jeremiah 30:17, Zechariah 9:12 & Romans 15:13

November 23

SONS NEEDED

Pilot Text: "…the creation eagerly waits for the revealing of the sons of God" – Romans 8:19

The whole of creation is waiting for sons, not children, to manifest. It is not just human beings that are waiting but the whole of creation. Every living thing is waiting for us to manifest as the sons of God. We are meant to teach and show the world how this earth is to be used from ecology to spirituality. But it will be sons that will be able to do this and not just children.

"…as many as received Him, to them gave He POWER TO BECOME the sons of God..." – John 1:12. He gives the power to BECOME the sons of God. To become means that you are not yet what you will become. When you receive Him by believing in Him, you instantaneously become a child of God but sonship is something that is grown into.

"…the heir, as long as he is a child, does not differ at all from a slave, though he is master of all…" – Galatians 4:1. You are an heir of all the benefits of salvation, but as long as you are a child, in practicality, you are no different from a slave. Potentially you are lord of all but unable to exercise your authority till you mature into your sonship.

"When I was a child, I spoke as a child, I understood as a child, I thought as a child; but when I became a man, I put away childish things." – 1 Corinthians 13:11. You must grow from childishness into maturity. No longer the subject, now the object; no longer the student, now the tutor; no longer the servant ,now the lord; NO LONGER THE CHILD, NOW THE SON.

How do you become a son? You must grow into your sonship. Today, determine to press towards maturity.

Key Thought: Grow from being a child to becoming a son. Sons are what the world has been waiting for.
Intelligent Prayer Point: Pray to grow and move from things of childhood to the maturity of sons.
Support Scriptures: Matthew 3:17, John 14:6 & Acts 4:11-13

November 24

THE RIGHT ENVIRONMENT FOR YOU

Pilot Text: 'In Him we live and move and have our being…' – Acts 17:28

God created man to be in His image and likeness. But before He created man, He created other things. This unveils a pattern with God. Before God creates a living thing, He creates the environment where the thing will live and thrive. And God makes sure that everything that living thing will need is in the environment He creates for it. EVERYTHING YOU NEED IS IN THE ENVIRONMENT GOD CREATED FOR YOU. You need to find your right environment.

God created the seas before He created the fish in the sea. He created the heavens before He created the birds in the heavens. He created the earth before He created the animals on the earth.

Also, in the creative process, we see that God speaks to the environment to give up the living thing that would live in it. So, He spoke to the seas to give up the fish, the heavens to give up the birds and the earth to give up the vegetation and the animals.

When God would create man, He did not speak to the seas, earth or sky, He spoke to Himself – 'Let us make man…' The real right environment for man is not the seas, earth or sky but God. God is meant to be your real right environment – 'in Him we live and move and have our being…' (Acts 17:28).

Everything you need is in the environment God created for you and created you for. When you take a living thing out of it's environment, it begins to die. When you step out from God, the process of death commences.

Get into the right environment today. Get into God.

Key Thought: You are created to dwell in the presence of God.
Intelligent Prayer Point: Pray that you will seek after God and dwell in His presence.
Support Scriptures: Genesis 1: 27 & Revelation 4:11

November 25

DO YOU HAVE THE RIGHT TO PRAY?

Pilot Text: '…the effective, fervent prayer of a righteous man avails much.' – James 5:16

Now, we understand that the status of the man that can pray effective, fervent, power producing prayer is that his is righteous. You need to be rooted and grounded in righteousness to function here. Israel had a zeal for God, but was ignorant of God's righteousness and sought to establish their own righteousness instead of submit to the righteousness of God (Romans 10:1-4). We have to be careful to not seek to establish our own righteousness by works, but rather, to submit to the righteousness of God, through faith.

The righteousness of God is a gift. You are justified by faith in Christ and thereby declared righteous. If you have accepted Christ, you are righteous. So, you must no longer approach prayer as an unworthy sinner, but now, as a righteous saint: approach clothed in His righteousness.

For too long, we have approached prayer with a sin consciousness and wondered why we didn't see much power released or answers received. When you approach as a sinner, you cannot be confident to receive much.

But now, I know who I am in Christ. I am the righteousness of God. I now approach with a righteousness consciousness. I come boldly to the throne of grace to obtain mercy and find grace in time of need. The only way you can come boldly to the throne of God and an innumerable company of angels is with a righteousness consciousness.

I am conscious of my righteousness. Are you? I am conscious of my RIGHTS-EOUSNESS. I am conscious of my RIGHTS in Christ. I have a right to healing. I have a right to prosperity. I have a right to direction. I have a right to elevation. I have a right to whatever the Word says I do. I have a right to answered prayers. Do you too?

Key Thought: Your right to answered prayers is your status of being the righteousness of God in Christ Jesus.
Intelligent Prayer Point: Pray for more knowledge and consciousness of your righteousness in Christ Jesus.
Support Scriptures: Romans 1:17, 2 Corinthians 5:21 & Hebrews 4:16

November 26

THIS IS YOUR VICTORY

Pilot Text: 'For whatsoever is born of God overcomes the world: and this is the victory that overcomes the world, even our faith.' – 1 John 5:4

Victory is what we have been promised. Victory is our destination. Jesus secured the victory for us through His death, burial and resurrection. But before we can realize the victory that has been guaranteed, we must still engage in battle. But this fight is a fight of faith. 'Fight the good fight of faith.' – 1 Timothy 6:12

Many things come against us in the world that we live in. We wake up daily to challenges and problems. But this is the victory that overcomes the world, even our faith. You have what it takes to win!

Our faith is our victory and our victory is our faith. Our faith is the substance of our victory. Our faith is the precursor to our victory and the victory itself. Our faith is our access to the victory.

'…you who have no money, come, buy and eat. Yes, come, buy wine and milk without money and without price.' – Isaiah 55:1. How do I buy without money? Because there is a different medium of exchange here. Faith is the currency of the kingdom of God. It is faith that you give, in exchange for anything in the kingdom of God. Your faith is the master key. Faith is central to the Kingdom. Everything in the kingdom is accessed by faith. Faith is the Operating System of the kingdom. Without faith nothing gets done!

FAITH IS NOT A SPARE TIRE that you bring out whenever you have a flat. Faith is all your tires and the fuel for the vehicle. Without faith, you are not going anywhere. Faith is the life that we live. '…the just shall live by His faith.' – Habakkuk 2:4

Go back to building your faith today; it is your victory!

Key Thought: Faith is key to your victory so, focus on building it up.
Intelligent Prayer Point: Pray for an increase in your faith, for victory in all areas of your life.
Support Scriptures: Romans 10:1, 2 Corinthians 5:7 & Ephesians 3:12

November 27

TOTAL VICTORY

Pilot Text: 'So David inquired of the Lord, saying, "Shall I pursue this troop? Shall I overtake them?" And He answered him, "Pursue, for you shall surely overtake them and without fail recover all.' – 1 Samuel 30:8

TOTAL RECOVERY is our portion. The Lord said pursue, you shall surely overtake and without fail recover all. TOTAL VICTORY IS YOUR PORTION.

God said to me that He is not done nor satisfied until your victory is complete and total. He does not deal in half measures. If it is not complete, He is not done yet. He came that we might have life and have life in its abundance, till it overflows. That is complete and total: that is TOTAL VICTORY.

'Count it all joy when you fall into various trials, knowing that the testing of your faith produces patience. But let patience have its perfect work, that you may be perfect and complete, lacking nothing.' – James 1:2-4. PERFECTION, COMPLETION AND LACKING NOTHING, IS THE END GAME.

When you understand this, you won't settle for less. Yes, you need patience because it might take time but don't stop till it is complete. Terah, Abram's Father set out to go to Canaan, but on the way, they settled in Haran. DON'T SETTLE. When Abram was of age, God called him to leave his Father's house – 'your Dad may have settled at Haran on the way to Canaan, but My intent to take you all the way to Canaan has not changed'.

When David caught up with those that had made away with his goods, the Scripture records 'nothing was missing, whether small or great, sons or daughters, spoil or anything that had been taken. David recovered all'.

NOTHING MISSING, NOTHING BROKEN, TOTAL VICTORY ALL THE WAY!

Key Thought: Don't settle for less, press into total victory in Christ.
Intelligent Prayer Point: Pray for the grace, strength and strategy to obtain total victory.
Support Scriptures: 1 Samuel 30:18,19, John 10:10 & 1 John 4:4

November 28

TRANSFORM DON'T CONFORM

Pilot Text: '…be not conformed to this world: but be ye transformed by the renewing of your mind…' – Romans 12:2

Jesus said 'GO into all the world'. This is our mandate to invade the world with the gospel of the kingdom of God. As we GO into the world, we must be aware that it is a dangerous place indeed. We are sent as sheep in the midst of wolves and must therefore be as wise as serpents yet gentle as doves (Matt. 10:16).

We must not fall in love with world for he that loves the world cannot love God at the same time (1 John 2:15). We must remember that though we are sent into the world we are not of the world (John 15:19, 17:16).
We must be conscious of the fact that we are meant to be the light of the world and not join the darkness (Matthew 5:14).

We need to beware of the enticements and seductions of the world. We are not called to conform to the world, but rather, to transform the world. You are called to make a difference, to be a change agent, to be a transformer.

True transformation does not start with others, but with you. It does not start in the world, but in you. It does not start outside, but inside. It does not start without, but within. 'As a man thinks, so he is… - Proverbs 23:7. Your internal environment ultimately determines your external environment. If you are going to change: if you are going to change your world, you have to change your thinking. '…BE TRANSFORMED BY THE RENEWING OF YOUR MIND…'

Transformation is not just wished for or prayed for. Real transformation is effected through thought. You can't keep thinking the same way and expect a different outcome. Controllers of thought control transformation.

Take charge of your thoughts today and don't conform to the world rather, transform it.

Key Thought: Personal transformation is the key to changing the world.
Intelligent Prayer Point: Pray that each day, you will walk in renewed mind and renewed life in Christ Jesus by the word of God.
Support Scriptures: Psalms 119:27, Mark 16:15 & Ephesians 4:22-24

November 29

SURROUNDED

Pilot Text: And when the servant of the man of God arose early and went out, there was an army, surrounding the city with horses and chariots. And his servant said to him, "Alas, my master! What shall we do?" – 2 Kings 6:15

Prophet Elisha and his servant were totally surrounded in the city of Dothan by the Syrian army. His servant panicked and cried 'what shall we do?'

Have you ever felt surrounded before? No way in and no way out. You can't see your way out or your way forward. Nothing can go out and nothing can come in. Internal demand exceeds external supply, creating internal tension and pent up frustration. Have you felt like pressure is building on the inside of you and there seems to be no outlet, no safe place to vent? Surrounded!

The servant panicked and thought they were done for, but soon noticed the calmness of his Prophet. Why was Elisha so calm? Why wasn't Elisha panicked and afraid? Couldn't He see that they were surrounded? What did he know that the servant did not? What could he see that his servant could not?

Elisha prayed that God open the eyes of his servant and immediately, he saw that there were, in fact, a greater army of heavenly horses and chariots of fire surrounding the army of the Syrians. So, what was surrounding Elisha and his servant was actually surrounded also. Elisha was in the center. So, what were surrounding him were not the armies of the enemies, but the armies of God. This meant that the Syrian army could do nothing that the armies of God did not allow.

This brings new light to Acts 17:28 which says 'in Him we live and move and have our being…' You are not surrounded by the enemy you are surrounded by God if you are in Christ. Hallelujah!

Key Thought: Your life is hid in Christ in God. You are divinely surrounded.

Intelligent Prayer Point: Pray to be more conscious of being divinely surround by God than any opponent.

Support Scriptures: Romans 8:31 & 1 John 4:4

November 30

THE STRUGGLE WITHIN

Pilot Text: Now Isaac pleaded with the Lord for his wife, because she was barren; and the Lord granted his plea, and Rebekah his wife conceived. But the children struggled together within her; and she said, "if all is well, why am I like this?" So she went to inquire of the Lord. – Genesis 25:21,22

(Excerpts from and inspired by the message 'The Tussle of the Twins' preached by Pastor Paul Adefarasin, Metropolitan of all House on The Rock Churches).

Rebekah had been barren and Isaac interceded on her behalf and she conceived. But now that she had been blessed with conception, she encountered a struggle within. She then asked 'if it be so, why am I thus?' - Genesis 25:22.

This is the contradiction of being blessed. When a blessing causes trouble. How can I be so blessed and still have these contradictions? If you are really blessed of God, you will have an internal struggle because of contradiction. If I am, indeed, carrying a blessing, why do I have so much trouble?'

Real prayer asks God questions. Real prayer asks "WHY?". Why do I have to have all this drama? Why me? Why now? Why not?

The truth is that in the birthing place of true greatness, there will always be great challenges. The contention is the proof of the huge stakes involved. Rebekah wondered at the struggle within her. She thought it was just the two children in her womb. But this was not just the tussle of twins; it was the tussle of two nations.

There is more at stake than you know. There is more being fought over than you are aware. The outcome of the internal contest have far reaching consequences; generations will be molded based on who wins that struggle going on inside you.

The struggle within is an age-old contention between two nations: Law and Grace, Esau and Jacob, Religion and Kingdom, Flesh and Spirit, Fear and Faith.

Who you feed, is who would win. So, which of the twins are you feeding?

Cry not at the struggle, it is only evidence of the greatness to be delivered. Feed the right twin and keep pushing. You will be delivered

Key Thought: Which ever twin you feed is the twin that would win.
Intelligent Prayer Point: Pray that you would put your self under and allow your spirit man ascendency.
Support Scriptures: 1 Kings 3:9, Philippians 1:9 & Hebrews 5:14

December 1

THERE IS ROOM FOR YOU

Pilot Text: 'A man's gift makes room for him, and brings him before great men.' – Proverbs 18:16

Often in this world, we feel as if there is not enough room for us. It is said that there is little space at the top. The more we attempt to rise, the more we encounter roadblocks and naysayers saying "there is no room here". Even Mary and Joseph found no space at the inns in Bethlehem.

We feel claustrophobic. We feel suffocated. We sometimes feel like the walls are closing in on us. We feel like we are being squeezed out. We feel pressed and squashed into ever shrinking rooms. We feel like there is no real room for us. Not accepted into the club. Not received into the business. Not endorsed for the job. Not approved for the relationship. NO ROOM!

But, I have come to contradict that report today. I came to tell you that there is room for you. There is a niche for you. There is a unique domain for you to occupy. Jesus said "occupy till I come". So, that means that there is a place for you to occupy. There is a space for you. THERE IS ROOM FOR YOU.

But, there is a key to your space: a key to your room. YOUR GIFT WILL MAKE ROOM FOR YOU. Your gift is your key to your space, in this world. You need to find your gift key. It is the key to your bigger room in this world.

'Do you see a man diligent and skillful in his business (GIFT)? He will stand before kings; he will not stand before obscure men.' – Proverbs 22:29. It is time to get busy with your gift today. It is going to take you higher than you imagined and bring you into places you only dreamed of. WORK THAT GIFT!

Key Thought: You cannot work your gift, unless you know it. Identify your gift!
Intelligent Prayer Point: Ask that the Holy Spirit open your eyes to your gift(s) and give you the wisdom to work it (them).
Support Scriptures: Romans 11:29, Romans 12:6 & 1 Corinthians 7:7

December 2

USE MY BOAT OH LORD

Pilot Text: '...they caught a great number of fish, and their net was breaking.' – Luke 5:6

When Simon obeyed the instruction of Jesus, he got a net-breaking and boat-sinking catch. Even today, God wants to bless you with a net-breaking and boat-sinking blessing.

As long as your blessing can be hidden, you are not yet blessed enough. God wants to bless you with the kind of blessing that you cannot hide. He wants your profiting to be evident to all (1 Timothy 4:15). He wants you planted in the house, yet flourishing in the courts (Psalms 92:13). He wants to bless you to the point where you cannot keep it to yourself. Simon had to call his partners to help with the catch. God wants to bless you to the point where you have to call your partners and friends, far and near, to share in the blessing.

But Simon's net-breaking and boat-sinking blessing was premised on him first, relinquishing his boat for Jesus' use. Simon's boat was his means of making a living. It was his life and his livelihood. Simon gave Jesus his boat (his life) to preach from.

Today, use my boat, Oh Lord. Preach from my boat. Teach from my boat. Make my boat a source of testimony. Use my boat, oh Lord! Use my car. Use my house. Use my wardrobe. Use my connections. Use my influence. Use my money. Use my experiences. Use my pain. Use my joy. Use my hands. Use my feet. Use my lips. Use my boat, Oh Lord!

God cannot bless what you do not release for His use.

Today say with me 'USE MY BOAT, OH LORD!'

Key Thought: You cannot release anything for His use and it would remain unblessed.
Intelligent Prayer Point: Pray for the spirit of surrender, that you may not withhold anything from God.
Support Scriptures: John 14:12, Galatians 2:20, Philippians 4:13 & Ephesians 2:10

December 3

WHAT ARE YOU SUPPLYING?

Pilot Text: '...the whole body, joined and knit together by what every joint supplies...' - Ephesians 4:16

The right place is not just about what the place is to you but also about what you are to the place. It is a two-way street. It is not just about what the place gives to you but also about what you give to the place.

'...the whole body, joined and knit together by what every joint supplies...' What are you supplying? When you withhold your supply you hinder growth and jeopardize unity. There is a demand for your supply. Find the demand for what you supply and you have gotten that much closer to finding your place.

It is not just about occupying space; it is about supplying in your place. When Jesus said occupy till I come He was not talking about treading water, he was talking about advancing, contributing and making impact.

It is time to contribute, bring something to the table, engage and be part of something great. It is not all about what you are going to get but more about what you are going to give. Interestingly, those that give more, get more.

When you just occupy space, you do the body a disservice – you don't allow others to really occupy the space and you don't really grow in the space. Your place is not static but a dynamic place of exchange: of demand and supply and vice versa. So, to occupy without really being occupied is tantamount to attempted sabotage. Ouch!

When you leave, what will be said about you? When you leave what will you be remembered for, or will you be remembered at all?

When your absence is not felt, then your presence was not needed.

Key Thought: Don't just occupy space, make sure you supply.
Intelligent Prayer Point: Pray that the Holy Spirit will help you cultivate a spirit of service, that you may go above and beyond, in supplying your part to the Body.
Support Scriptures: Ephesians 4:11-16, Colossians 3:23 & 1 Peter 4:10a

December 4

FAITH PRAISE

Pilot Text: 'And at midnight Paul and Silas prayed, and sang praise unto God: and the prisoners heard them.' – Acts 16:25

In the midnight hour, with many reasons to be disheartened, discouraged and depressed. Locked up with their hands in chains, feet in stocks and backs bleeding, yet, Paul and Silas prayed and praised. How do you do that? It had to be faith praise. By the spirit of faith, they vacated their current prison and took up dwelling in the promises of God, so they could give God praise in advance!

We cannot step into the greater without faith. The greater is for the faithful and the faith-full.

The Scriptures record that the prisoners in other cells heard their praise. Their praise was not the silent kind. The truth is, faith does not hide. Faith is audible and visible. Paul and Silas' praise was not silent praise within their hearts. There's nothing wrong with private praise, but praise is sweetest when others can hear it. To praise in the presence of others is to display no shame. If you hide your praise for God then maybe you are ashamed of Him.

Their praise was not a function of their feelings. They did not feel like praising God. They were in pain and in restrictions. But they praised anyway. WILL YOU PRAISE GOD ANYWAY. The other prisoners in other cells heard their praise. LET OTHERS HEAR YOUR PRAISE TODAY! (Stop withholding your testimony, it is part of your praise!).

Faith praise always makes something happen. Psalms 22:3 says God inhabits the praises of Israel. Faith praise creates an attractive habitation for God. Paul and Silas' sacrificial praise was a sweet smelling aroma to God and a habitation that attracted Him. As God took up residence in their praise, the prison was too small to contain Him; there was an earthquake and every door opened and all restraints were broken.

As you offer faith praise today, the MIDNIGHT HOUR GOD OF SUDDENLY will show up!

Your faith praise will shake age-old foundations of evil that have held you imprisoned. As you give God faith praise, doors will open and access will be granted to where you could not go before. Chains will be loosed and true freedom will be yours. WHY NOT GIVE GOD FAITH PRAISE TODAY?

Key Thought: Praise in the midst of contradictory circumstances can only be by faith.
Intelligent Prayer Point: Pray that the spirit of faith will rise strong in you to praise God even in trouble.
Support Scriptures: Psalms 22:3, 149:5,6 & Habakkuk 3:17-19

December 5

WHAT TIME IS IT?

Pilot Text: 'And of the children of Issachar, which were men that had understanding of the times, to know what Israel ought to do...' – 1 Chronicles 12:32

The imperative of knowing what time it is cannot be underestimated. What makes an action wise or foolish is determined by WHEN the action is taken. So, wisdom is not only 'why' but 'when'. What time is it?

What distinguished the sons of Issachar from others was their understanding of times. They knew what time it was. As a result, they knew what ought to be done and had their brethren at their command.

When you don't know what time it is, you won't know what you ought to do. When you don't know what time it is, you run the high risk of doing the wrong thing. When you don't know what time it is, you will be at the command of others. It is a vital question to ask often. WHAT TIME IS IT?

An understanding of the times includes a grasp of 'chronos' and 'kairos'. 'Chronos' is the continuous passage of time from second to second, while 'kairos' are opportune times within 'chronos'. You have to remain alert and vigilant in 'chronos' to catch 'kairos'. There will be many 'kairos' moments when the heavens meet the earth in this year. You must be ready to seize the moments.

What time is it? We are in dark times. We are in the end times. We are in challenging times. We live in evil days. But, these are also opportune times. For in darkness the light shines.

It is time to be plugged deeper into God. It is time to be under godly authority. It is time to be planted and not roving. It is time to run with the vision. It is time to serve faithfully. It is time to give, on another level. It is time to…

Key Thought: Knowing what time it is, is vital for your advance.
Intelligent Prayer Point: Pray for a discerning spirit to know your Kairos moments and wisdom to seize them.
Support Scriptures: Ecclesiastes 3:1 & 1 Thessalonians 5:1

December 6

WHEN GOD COMES DOWN

Pilot Text: 'But the Lord came down…' – Genesis 11:5

When God comes down everything changes. God came down in Genesis 11 and dealt with the self-centered plans of men. He tampered with their language, confused their speech and dissolved their unity. God came down, again, in Acts 2, similar to Genesis 11 but very different. In both instances, the people spoke in new tongues but the outcome was remarkably different. In one, disunity, in the other, unity.

In Genesis, they sought to make a name for themselves, but in Acts, they sought to proclaim the name of Jesus. In Genesis, it was all about self, but in Acts it was all about God.

In Genesis, they wanted to build a city, but in Acts, they wanted God to invade the city. In Genesis, they wanted to build a tower to reach the heavens, but in Acts, the heavens came to the earth.

In Genesis, they built with bricks, but in Acts, they were the lively stones being built into the house of God (1 Peter 2:5).

In Genesis, they did not want to be scattered abroad, but in Acts, they were scattered abroad to be witnesses of the Christ in Jerusalem, Judea, Samaria and unto the ends of the earth.

In Genesis, their unity was established on uniformity, but in Acts, their unity was in the midst of diversity. In Genesis, what bound them together was external, but in Acts, what bound them together was spiritual. In Genesis, their imagination was shut down, but in Acts, their imagination was unleashed.

The difference was, in Genesis they sought to advance without God while in Acts, they waited for God. But one thing is guaranteed: when God comes down, everything changes. We need God to come down like He did in Acts, again.

WHEN GOD COMES DOWN, HE DOESN'T TAKE SIDES, HE TAKES OVER.

May God come down in your life's situations today!

Key Thought: When God comes down, everything changes.
Intelligent Prayer Point: Pray that God will come down in your life, causing every adverse situation to melt like wax.
Support Scriptures: Psalms 68:1,2 & Isaiah 64:1-4

December 7

YOU CAN WALK ON WATER TOO

Pilot Text: 'Now in the fourth watch of the night Jesus went to them, walking on the sea'. – Matthew 14:25

One way to handle a storm is to keep the water out of your boat. To keep the water out of your boat you have to keep your eyes on Jesus. Another way to handle a storm is to learn to walk on water. If you keep your eyes on Jesus, the water cannot get into your boat. If you keep your eyes on Jesus, you can walk on water too!

The other day, Jesus was walking on water and His disciples saw Him and were afraid. Peter said if it is you bid me come. Jesus said come and Peter stepped out and walked on water (Matthew 14:22-32). SOMETIMES YOU JUST HAVE TO STEP OUT!

The Bible says that when Peter SAW the winds and the waves boisterous, he feared and began to sink. WHEN HE SAW. He had to have taken his eyes off Jesus in order to see the winds and the waves. Don't take your eyes off the master! When you take your eyes off Jesus, you allow water into the boat of your heart and you'll start to sink.

Don't worry about the winds and the waves. All you need to be concerned about is, DID HE SAY "COME"? If He said it, that settles it. If He said "come". If He said "Let's go over to the other side". If He said "start it". If He said "give it". He is committed to completing whatever He starts. 'Looking onto Jesus, the author and finisher of our faith…' – Hebrews 12:2

Numbers 23:19 – 'God is not a man that He should lie; neither the son of man that He should repent: hath he said, and shall He not do it? Or hath He spoken, and shall He not make it good?'
It is time to step out of the safety of your comfort zone and walk on water. It is time to walk on what has been walking on you. DON'T LET WATER IN YOUR BOAT. KEEP YOUR EYES ON JESUS. YOU CAN WALK ON WATER TOO!

Key Thought: It is time to walk on what has been walking on you.
Intelligent Prayer Point: Pray that your gaze will be fixed on God's Word and God's Word alone.
Support Scriptures: Hebrews 12:1 & 1 Chronicles 29:18

December 8

SHALL GOD'S WILL BE DONE?

Pilot Text: "Your kingdom come. Your will be done on earth as it is in heaven." – Matthew 6:10

Shall God's will be done?
If God's immediate will would done no matter what, He would not tell us to pray 'Your will be done on earth as it is in heaven'. So, mostly God's will is not done on the earth unless we pray for and submit to it.

God's will is not done but will yet be done! In the final day His Will shall be done in judgment. But God is only in control in the earth to the degree that He is given control.

Why is this distinction important?
As much as we draw a lot of consolatory strength and hope from believing that God is in control and that His Will shall be done, we need to be careful of the negative fall-out when this belief is not held in balance. This belief could lull you to sleep and absolve you of any sense of responsibility for your world.

Understanding that God's will won't automatically be done and that God's immediate control of circumstances is to the degree that we allow Him control, awakens us to responsibility for our world. If His will shall be done on earth as in heaven, it will be because someone on earth is insisting that it be done.

All the evil in the world is not His will, but the consequences of the exercise of human will in conjunction with Satanic schemes.

It is time for you and me, through our prayers and actions, to insist on the Will of God to be done in our world.

So, I ask you today, 'shall God's will be done in your world?'

Key Thought: The will of God is not automatic, but must be insisted on by us.
Intelligent Prayer Point: Insist that the will of God be done in your life.
Support Scriptures: Luke 22:42, Mark 11:25 & Acts 21:14

December 9

THANK MEN BUT GIVE GLORY TO GOD

Pilot Text: "…one of them… turned back… glorified God… giving him thanks…" – Luke 17:15,18

Ten lepers were healed but only one came back to give thanks. The one that came back to give thanks was not just cleansed but was made whole. He came with the intent to thank Jesus and give glory to God. There is an important lesson to be learnt here.

This leper realized that his healing didn't just drop from the sky. Someone had been used to bring this blessing into his life. So, as much as He gave the glory to God, he went back to say thank you to the vessel used. We too must learn to do both.

Sometimes, we are super spiritual and ignore the men that God uses to bless us saying we are giving glory to God alone. This is not right.
In fleshy attempts to keep men humble, we bypass saying "thank you" to them because all glory must be to God. This, again, is not right. It is not your job to keep any man humble but yourself. Thank men but give glory to God.
Men are worthy of thanks but only God is deserving of glory. Don't rob men of their thanks because even God is not happy with that.

Live a life of thanksgiving. Thank the men that God uses to bless you, inspire you, help you, lift you and encourage you. Lay it to heart to say "thank you", but give glory to God because, He is the true source off all good things. Acknowledge the conduit and glorify the source. If that man had not availed himself of God's use, God might have used someone else but there might have been a delay.

Today, thank the men who have blessed you, but give the glory to God.

Key Thought: Thanks to men and glory to God.
Intelligent Prayer Point: Pray for a thankful heart and a discerning spirit to return all glory to God, the giver of life.
Support Scriptures: Psalms 30:11-12, Psalms 107:20-22 & 1 Timothy 1:17

December 10

THE GATES WILL NOT PREVAIL

Pilot Text: "…I will build my church, and the gates of Hades shall not prevail against it." – Matthew 16:18

Gates are significant. Gates grant or deny access. The gates of a city can determine the flow of commerce and the economy of the city. He who owns the gates owns the city. In ancient Israel, gates were also where policies, strategies and judgments were determined. The elders sat at the gate, not to while away time, but to determine how to move things forward. So, the gates of hell are the schemes, strategies, judgments and plots of hell. So, when He says the gates of hell shall not prevail against you, He is saying the schemes, strategies, judgments and plots of hell will not succeed against you.

Have you ever had a scary dream where gates were chasing you? Most likely not. Gates are stationary and do not chase people. So, when He says the gates will not prevail against you, it is not the gates that are on the move, they are stationary, you are the one meant to be on the move against the gates.

Gates are defensive structures, not offensive. We are the ones meant to be on the offensive against the gates of hell. So, if the gates of hell are prevailing against you, maybe it is because you have taken a defensive position instead of an offensive one. It is time to go on the offensive. Storm the gates of hell to take back everything the devil stole.

I have a sure promise: the gates of hell cannot prevail. So, I am putting on my heavenly armor and coming against the gates to reverse every judgment of hell and take back all the devil stole. I'm taking my joy back. I'm taking my peace back. I'm taking my prosperity back. I'm taking my progress back. I'm taking back all that the devil stole. What about you?

Key Thought: The gates of hell will not prevail against the offensive believer.
Intelligent Prayer Point: Ask God to help you take your stand in Him, as you take back all that hades snatched from you.
Support Scriptures: Psalms 129:2, Isaiah 22:22, John 16:10 & 1 Corinthians 15:57

December 11

TO DRINK OR NOT TO DRINK

Pilot Text: "...the master of the feast... tasted the water that was made wine..."John 2:9

Jesus turned water into wine. Was this an endorsement for wine drinking? Doesn't the Bible forbid the saints from drinking alcohol? Does it? Well I have not yet found a Scripture that directly says do not drink wine. But Proverbs 20:1 says "Wine is a mocker, strong drink is a brawler, and whoever is led astray by it is not wise". Though the Bible might not say directly don't drink alcohol, it does say if you want to be mocked, indulge in wine; if you want to be a brawler, embrace strong drink; and if you want to be classified under those that are not wise, make alcohol your friend.

The Bible uses wine as an analogy often. The wine often used as an analogy, is not the nonalcoholic type. Ephesians 5:18 says 'do not be drunk with wine, in which is dissipation; but be filled with the Spirit'. To say 'do not be drunk' means it's the type of wine that you can be drunk on. The essential alternative to wine for the Believer is to be full of the Spirit of God.

So, though I cannot find a Scripture that says it is a sin to taste wine, it is clearly unwise and does not bring glory to God. Also, as you mature as a Believer, you will find that you cannot indulge in what others permit, for the sake of your consecration and to be a vessel of honor the Lord can use anytime. (Some of us, as spiritual Nazarenes, do not touch alcohol at all).

As a holy nation and a royal priesthood, we cannot be under the influence of alcohol and have our judgment impaired by wine. Though it might be lawful (defendable) it is not expedient (beneficial across board). Also, for the faith of others, we refrain from what we can justify.

So, do not be drunk with earthly wine, rather, be filled with the new wine of the Spirit.

Key Thought: The Bible does directly forbid drinking wine but says, do not get drunk with it, rather be full of the spirit.
Intelligent Prayer Point: Pray to be full of the Spirit and right judgment at all times and in all matters.
Support Scriptures: Proverbs 31:4, Matthew 27:34 & Romans 14:20

December 12

IN YOUR HANDS

Pilot Text: "Then God said, let us make man in our image, according to our likeness; let them have dominion…" – Genesis 1:26

In the beginning God said 'Let us… let them'. The implications of this statement are far reaching. This was the delegation of authority to man; however, there can be no authority without responsibility. If you would have authority, you must embrace responsibility too; they go hand in hand. By this statement, God was placing the authority (and responsibility) for the earth in the hands of man. From this point onwards, to get anything done on the earth, you would have to go through man.

Now, even God needed man's permission or authorization to intervene in the earth for the period of man's lease on the earth. It is not a lack of ability on the part of God, but He would not break His word so He waits for the legal premise to intervene, God is waiting on you.

We give God the permission to intervene through our prayers. So, prayer becomes our pathway to give God access and permission to intervene in our situations and circumstances. Myles Munroe puts it this way – "prayer is earthly license for heavenly interference."

Satan understands this power of prayer hence, he fights hard to keep you from praying. When you pray, you allow God in; the power is in your hands. Commit to pray everyday today.

Key Thought: Prayer is your legal premise for divine intervention.
Intelligent Prayer Point: Pray that God will intervene in all your life circumstances.
Support Scriptures: Genesis 9:1-2, Psalms 115:16 & Hebrews 2:7-8

December 13

A MUSTARD SEED & A MOUNTAIN

Pilot Text: '…" Because of your unbelief; for assuredly, I say to you, if you have faith as a mustard seed, you will say to this mountain, 'Move from here to there,' and it will move; and nothing will be impossible for you.' – Matthew 17:20

In response to the disciples request for an increase in faith, Jesus said if you have faith as a mustard seed you can achieve the impossible (Luke 17:5,6). So, the problem is not the size of your faith, but rather, the strength of your faith.

But, what determines the strength of your faith? Nourishment and use are important determinants of the development of strength. What will be strong must be nourished and used (exercised).

Another determinant of the strength of your faith is the presence or absence of doubt (unbelief). In every injunction to do the impossible through faith, there is an admonishment to not doubt or entertain unbelief. So, the strength and efficiency of your faith is determined by the absence or presence of doubt. It is not really the size of your faith that is the issue, but rather, the presence of doubt.

In other words, A mustard seed of faith can move a mountain in the absence of doubt and a mountain of faith can move nothing in the presence of doubt. A mustard seed of doubt can stop a mountain of faith and a mountain of doubt cannot stop a mustard seed of faith that does not doubt. [Selah – think about it…].

What you really need to deal with is your doubt. How? Feed your faith and starve your doubt. Again how? Give your ears to the Word of God that feeds faith and shut your ears to the report of the devil, to starve your doubt.
Release the power of mustard seed faith today by eliminating doubt!

Key Thought: The issue is not the size, but the strength of your faith.
Intelligent Prayer Point: Uproot fear, doubt and unbelief out of your heart in prayer.
Support Scriptures: Mark 11:23-24 & Luke 17:5,6

December 14

LOSS OF FAITH IN PRAYER

Pilot Text: "Ask, and it will be given to you; seek, and you will find; knock, and it will be opened to you." – Matthew 7:7

Prayer is our power with God; little prayer, little power; much prayer, much power; no prayer, no power. But the problem with this generation is, we have lost faith in the power of prayer. Because many have so lost their faith in prayer, they now attempt to do things by themselves, in their own strength. They say "I prayed and nothing happened, so I took matters into my own hands." What they fail to realize is that faith without works (corresponding action) is dead, so, prayer without action is not complete. Your prayers should lead to some form of faith-action on your part.

Prayer without action is equivalent to laziness and irresponsibility. Those that only pray and never take corresponding action see little or no results and then conclude that prayer does not work.

Action without prayer equals self-righteousness and pride. When all we have is action and no prayer, we end up full of arrogance, pride and self-righteousness because, we conclude that anything we achieve is by our own action. When you do not pray, your confidence remains only in your actions.

To pray is to admit need for help and acknowledge power beyond you. To pray is to submit to the sovereignty of God. Be wary of the seduction of your competence because it cannot replace the necessity of prayer. Prayer with corresponding action always brings results. It is time to combine both for results in your life's situations.

Key Thought: Not adding action to your prayer of faith, leads to no answers.
Intelligent Prayer Point: Pray for the resolve to add the right corresponding actions to your faith
Support Scriptures: Psalm 65:2, Jeremiah 29:13 & Mark 11:24

December 15

THE THREE 'D's OF PRAYER

Pilot Text: 'Therefore I say unto you, what things soever ye desire, when ye pray, believe that ye receive them, and ye shall have them.' – Mark 11:24

There are three Ds necessary for an effective prayer life. The first is the DESIRE for prayer. Desire is the starting place for effective prayer. You need to learn to harness the power of desire to fuel your prayers. Desire is so important that God will allow situations in your life to create desire for prayer within you. The trouble in your life was meant to fuel your desire to pray; you have to cultivate the desire for prayer.

After Desire comes the DISCIPLINE of prayer. Desire alone is not enough. You need to add the DISCIPLINE of prayer to your Desire for prayer. The proof of desire is pursuit and your discipline reveals your pursuit. You have not prayed till you have prayed!

After the desire for prayer comes the discipline of prayer. The discipline of prayer leads to the DELIGHT of prayer. This is when prayer becomes a delight. The delight of prayer often comes when you start to see the answers to your prayers: when you start to see the power of your prayers and your power with God.

The Delight of prayer fuels the cycle of prayer because the delight of prayer creates even greater desire for prayer, which in turn causes the development of more discipline for prayer and yet more delight. A positive cycle of prayer is set in motion.

But, there is yet a higher level of delight. Where the delight is not coming necessarily from the answers but from the pleasure of His presence. At this level, I no longer come in for what He can do or give, but I come for who He is.

Key Thought: To pray effectively, you need desire for, discipline of and delight of prayer.
Intelligent Prayer Point: Pray that the desire, discipline and delight of prayer will be birthed in you through the help of the Holy Spirit.
Support Scriptures: Proverbs 15:8, Psalms 66:20 & Zechariah 12:10

December 16

TONGUES OF FIRE

Pilot Text: "And suddenly there came a sound from heaven as of a rushing mighty wind, and it filled all the house where they were sitting. And there appeared unto them cloven tongues like as of fire, and it sat upon each of them. And they were all filled with the Holy Ghost, and began to speak with other tongues, as the Spirit gave them utterance" – Acts 2:2-4

The Holy Spirit fell as a rushing mighty wind and they were all filled with the Spirit and there were tongues of fire on each of them. There is a tongue of fire and a unique anointing of the Spirit for you. All were filled with the Spirit, but each with his own tongue of fire. It is time for you to embrace your uniqueness and what you uniquely bring to the table, in the anointing of the Spirit.

Tongues speak; your tongue will speak. Your anointing will be heard. But you have to be filled with the Holy Spirit and stay faithful to what you are called to. The Spirit gave utterance, but they did the speaking. The Spirit will give you utterance, but you have to speak; He will give the unction, but you have to function. The spirit will give the anointing, but you have to go forward!

Some days later the disciples were told to stop preaching the gospel. They went to God and said "Lord, behold their threatenings…" and they were all filled with the Holy Spirit and spoke the word of God with boldness (Acts 4:29-31). I don't know what threatening you are facing right now. Maybe you are threatened that this year would not end well for you. When you allow the Spirit fall on you, all threatenings will cease; you will prevail!

Key Thought: Tongues rule the world. Get your tongues of fire to rule your world.
Intelligent Prayer Point: Today, ask for the anointing of the Spirit to come on you and for your unique tongue to find expression.
Support Scriptures: Matthew 3:11, Acts 1:5 & Acts 4:31

December 17

UNITY And VISION

Pilot Text: "And the Lord said, behold, the people is one, and they have all one language; and this they begin to do: and now nothing will be restrained from them, which they have imagined (envisioned) to do" – Genesis 11:6.

In other words, God said these people's vision will be fulfilled because they are united. Unity enables vision; successful vision is irrevocably connected to unity. Vision galvanizes unity and unity is essential for vision. Vision gives us something to be united about and our unity around it, actualizes it.

Vision gives focus to unity. Without vision, unity is difficult, whether on an individual or corporate level. On the other hand, vision cannot be achieved without unity; they have to work together. Scripture says "unless the eye be single..." (Matthew 6:22-23); this means unless the eye is focused, there will be chaos. Unless the vision be a unit (all one), success will be elusive. So for success we must master both unity and vision. When we are all one, there is no vision that we cannot achieve.

On an individual level, this means that you focus all your attributes on your vision and are not double-minded. You bring all you have to bear on your vision. On a corporate level, we all come together around a vision, to see that vision fulfilled.

Ponder the following: Division is double vision; vision is a unit; division is disunity; successful vision in effect is unity. If you can become a unit (as an individual or as a group), you will actualize vision. If you find unity, you have found vision. If you find vision, you have found the premise for unity.

Key Thought: Vision and unity work hand in hand for the fulfillment of destiny.
Intelligent Prayer Point: Pray for unity in the body of Christ, so that we are able to achieve all that God will have us do here on the earth.
Support Scriptures: Genesis 13:8, Psalms 133:1 & Luke 11:34

December 18

VISION OR AMBITION?

Pilot Text: "And they said, Go to, let us build us a city and a tower, whose top may reach unto heaven; and let us make us a name, lest we be scattered abroad upon the face of the whole earth" – Genesis 11:4

There are many grand endeavors on the face of the earth. But the question is, "are these products of vision or ambition?" There are many things we call great vision, which actually, from a God perspective, are just great ambitions.

Vision and ambition can be confused with each other, because they can look alike. Many great men of God have been accused of being ambitious yet burning in their hearts was only a godly vision that would not let them sleep. It is important to determine, on a personal level, whether yours is a God-given vision or a self-driven ambition. How?

In Genesis 11, the people gathered to do something great on the earth, but their motivation was ambition. They said "let us make us a name". This speaks to the heart of ambition. Ambition is about self; it is self-centered. They sought to make a name for themselves when, in the very next chapter, God said to Abram, "I will make your name great". God has no problem with great names. His issue is with who makes the name great: him or you, vision or ambition?

Vision is about others, it is empowering and is a blessing. Where ambition is focused on self, vision is focused on others. Where ambition wants to take, vision wants to give. Where ambition tries to exclude others, vision tries to include others. Where ambition seeks to compete, vision seeks to complement. The interesting thing is that true vision is always bigger than ambition.

So, what are you pursuing, vision or ambition?

Key Thought: True vision is always bigger than ambition.
Intelligent Prayer Point: Pray that you will have the right perspective and correct vision.
Support Scriptures: 2 Samuel 8:13, Proverbs 10:7 & Matthew 26:31

December 19

WHAT DO YOU EXPECT?

Pilot Text: "And a certain man lame from his mother's womb was carried, whom they laid daily at the gate of the temple which is called Beautiful to ask alms of them that entered the temple. Who seeing Peter and John, asked for alms. And Peter fastening his eyes upon him with John, said: look at us. And he gave heed to them expecting to receive something of them…" – Acts 3:2-5.

The end of this story has this lame man totally healed and restored to perfect soundness. But, one of the triggers to his miracle was his expectation. The Scriptures said he gave them his attention expecting to receive something. Expectation is key to manifestation.

But your expectation is governed by your perception. In his hometown, Jesus could not perform many mighty works because there was no expectation. This was because they did not perceive Him as one who could do such for them. They only saw him as the carpenter's son. Scripture says: "He who receives a prophet in the name of a prophet shall receive a prophet's reward"– Matthew 10:41.

Familiarity can rob you of the right perception; your expectation is governed by your perception. So, you will not expect anything significant and will not receive anything of note. The other day someone asked me to lend him $4000. Though I did not have the money, it told me his perception of me. So, his request did not upset me because it was actually a complement. I had made his shortlist of persons that must have excess of the amount he requested (in his perception).

You do not ask anyone for something that you do not expect that they have. So, your request is a revelation of your estimation of the person. If I did not think you could do it, I would not ask you for it. So, what have you asked God for lately? Is it possible that your request of God is a revelation of your true estimation of what God can do in your life's situation? Or has life battered you so much that you have recalibrated your expectations downwards?

Today, He is saying "let it be to you according to your faith" (expectation). What can He not do? Nothing… nothing is impossible with Him.

Key Thought: Expectation is key to manifestation. Get your expectations right!
Intelligent Prayer Point: Pray that your expectation will be aligned with the possibilities in the will of God.
Support Scriptures: 1 Kings 17:9-15, 20-24 & Matthew 7:8

December 20

A MIRACLE AT A BEAUTIFUL GATE

Pilot Text: "And a certain man lame from his mother's womb was carried, whom they laid daily at the gate of the temple which is called Beautiful, to ask alms from those who entered the temple." – Acts 3:2

Peter and John were going up to the temple at the hour of prayer. Peter and John were committed to prayer: personal and corporate prayer. They went up to pray. The miracle happened on their way to prayer. Miracles happen on the way to prayer. Commit to prayer and you'll meet your miracle on the way.

The lame man was at a beautiful gate: an ugly situation at a beautiful gate. This is often our reality: Ugly problems in a beautiful Church, disgruntled people in a palatial setting, looking good on the outside but a mess on the inside, the best and the worst of times at the same time, seated in heavenly places but living on earth…ugly situations at beautiful gates.

Peter said "look on us". For the lame man to look on them, he had to look up. This was an instruction to raise his expectation. Expectation is the key to manifestation. Expectations are the first embers of victorious faith. Look up. Raise your expectations. Awaken your faith.

Peter then said 'silver and gold I do not have…rise up and walk'. He was saying, don't limit yourself to natural solutions. Don't let the lack of silver and gold stop you. God can do it without the normal means. God can still blow your mind and exceed your expectations.

Get up and walk. Stop sitting down waiting for something to happen. Get up and make it happen. Faith without works is dead. Get up and get to work.

When Peter said 'rise up and walk', nothing happened for a moment. Peter then grabbed him by the hand and lifted him up and the miracle took place. Sometimes, you need to take it a step further and take it by force.

MIRACLES ARE WAITING AT BEAUTIFUL GATES, IF WE TAKE THEM BY FORCE.

Take it by force: apply the keys today.

Key Thought: Expectation is key to manifestation. Miracles are waiting on the other side of expectation.
Intelligent Prayer Point: Ask God to help you recognize your miracle when it comes your way, and faith to reach out take it.
Support Scriptures: Psalms 77:14, Mark 11:24 & Hebrews 11:1

December 21

YOU ARE GREAT

Pilot Text: No longer shall your name be called Abram, but your name shall be Abraham; for I have made you a father of many nations. – Genesis 17:5

Abram means 'exalted father' while Abraham means 'father of a multitude'. For 99 years, Abraham was known as Abram. He carried with him, the promise of offspring, but for 99 years, he was without a child from Sarai. But then, God changed his name. Within a year of the name change, they had Isaac.

A name represents an identity. God had to update Abram's identity to get the blessing through to him. Your sense of identity is critical. Satan knows this, hence often, his first port of attack is your identity. Eve fell for it and attempted to become, by works, what she already was, by grace. Satan came again to Jesus and said, 'if you are the son of God turn these stones to bread'. This temptation was a question of identity. If Jesus had fallen for it and turned the stones to bread, it would have indicated that he doubted his identity. But Jesus did not fall for it. You cannot afford to be confused about your identity. Jesus knew who He was and is. You've got to know who you are. I know who I am.

Who determines identity? The father of a child determines the child's identity. You get your identity from your father. Who's your daddy now? To know your identity, you have got to know your father. You carry the DNA of your father. If you are a child of the Most High, then you carry His DNA and… Psalms 82:6 – '…You are gods; and all of you are children of the most High.'

If He is mighty, you are mighty. If He is wise, you are wise. If He is strong, you are strong. Whatever He is, you are. If He is great, then you are great.

To walk in the greater that God has for you and I, we must come to terms with our true identity in God. I am great. You are great. We are great!

You might have stumbled and sinned, but that does not make you a sinner, you are still a saint. A sinner is one who habitually sins, because that is his nature. That you failed does not make you a failure. You are really a success who went through a failure-class to learn what works and what doesn't work. That you messed up doesn't make you a mess up. You are a message that had to go through a mess to add to your age, to make it a message.

You cannot afford to define your identity by what you go through. You define your identity by who gave birth to you. And if any man be in Christ, he is born of God.

So today, regardless of what you face, walk with a conviction and consciousness that YOU ARE GREAT!

Key Thought: Your true identity is determined by your heavenly Father.
Intelligent Prayer Point: Pray that you would not fall for any deceptions of the devil causing you to doubt your true identity in God.
Support Scriptures: Matthew 5:13-16, John 10:34,35 & 1 Peter 2:9,10

December 22

THE RIGHT PLACE

Pilot Text: "Those who are planted in the house of the Lord shall flourish in the courts of our God." – Psalm 92:13

There is nothing wrong with a square peg, neither is there anything wrong with a round hole. They are just incompatible. Put square pegs in square holes and round pegs in round holes and not vice versa. You have to find your place.

Let me re-emphasize, once again, that there is a place for you. Square peg, there is a place for you. Round peg, there is a place for you. Whatever-peg you are, there is a place for you. Your existence is proof that there is a hole shaped and fashioned for you.

The right place is the house of God. David understood that the right place was the house of God so, he said "one thing have I desired and that will I seek after that I might dwell in the house of the Lord all the days of my life" (Psalms 27:4).

You have to be planted in the house of God. It is not enough to visit the right place. You have to make it your dwelling place. What is not planted does not grow. If you are not planted, you will not grow. When you are planted in the house, you will flourish in the courts. When you are faithful in God's house, you will prevail in the world.

The right place is where the Word of God is delighted in. The right place is where the rivers of God's Word and revelation are flowing. The right place is where there is sincere worship. The right place is where the presence of God is. The right place is where you are blessed, but challenged; lifted, yet provoked; encouraged, also motivated; inspired and driven. It's time for you to find your right place in the house of the Lord.

Key Thought: Finding the right place is essential for your spiritual growth.
Intelligent Prayer Point: Pray for divine direction and confirmations of the right place for you.
Support Scriptures: Psalms 48:2, John 10:35 & 1 Corinthians 14:26

December 23

LOSE IT TO FIND IT

Pilot Text: "He who finds his life will lose it, and he who loses his life for My sake will find it." – Matthew 10:39

The most important discovery after discovering God, is to discover yourself in Him. However, you must find God first, because the purpose of a thing can only be authentically found in the mind of its creator. Find God, then find you. GET LOST IN GOD AND YOU'LL FIND YOUR TRUE SELF, IN HIM.

So, to find your life, you have to lose your life. Lose it to find it. You have to give it away to truly own it. If you can't give it away, you don't really own it yet, maybe it owns you. When Simon found out who Christ was, he then found out who he was: no longer Simon but Peter (Matthew 16:16,17)

TRUE SELF DISCOVERY IS IN GOD DISCOVERY.

You are not a mistake. You were born on purpose, for a purpose. Before the creation of a thing, a need was identified that necessitated the creation of the thing to meet the need. So, the need preceded the creation of the thing. There is a need that you are designed to meet. There is a question you answer. A problem you solve. A sickness you heal. A pain you alleviate. A unique flavor you bring to the mix.

Paul prayed that he would 'apprehend that for which he was apprehended' (Philippians 3:12). There is a reason you were apprehended. The purpose of your salvation is far more than just to go to heaven. After at least 15 years of active ministry, Paul was still talking about apprehending his purpose and knowing Christ and the power of His resurrection.

THE PURSUIT OF PURPOSE IS A LIFETIME PURSUIT.

Purpose is not revealed in its totality at once, but progressively as you pursue. Don't be frustrated that you do not know it all now rather, rejoice that you are on the journey.

LOSE IT TO FIND IT!

Key Thought: To find your life and true purpose, you must be willing to lose it for the sake of the gospel.
Intelligent Payer Point: Pray that you would let go and let God.
Support Scriptures: Matthew 16:24-25, Mark 8:35 & Philippians 2:3-5

December 24

ZACHARIAS VS MARY

This is an angelic season.

Hebrews 1:14 tells us that angels are all ministering spirits, sent forth to minister for them who shall be heirs of salvation?). They are heavenly couriers of messages and blessings from on high.

Angels, we have heard on high, but they speak not of themselves, but of Christ our King. HOW WILL YOU RESPOND, WITH FAITH OR WITH DOUBT?

Angel Gabriel appeared to Zacharias and told him that his elderly wife would have a son and he responded 'HOW SHALL I KNOW THIS…? (Luke 1:18). Angel Gabriel appeared to Mary and told her that she would bear the son of God and she responded 'HOW SHALL THIS BE…? (Luke 1:38). Their answers seem similar if not the same. But a closer look reveals that they were not.

Zacharias asked how he would know it. In other words, he did not believe. He needed a sign. His question revealed his unbelief. He was given a sign. He was made dumb till John was born. The other reason he was made dumb was so he could not use the unbelief in his mouth to abort the miracle.

Mary's question was "how shall this be?". This was not an indication of doubt, but rather, an inquisition into the process for the working of the miracle. God is not afraid of your questions on process as long as they are still coming from a place of faith. Mary believed the Word, but only wanted to know how it would happen. Gabriel told her the how. He said the Holy Spirit would come upon her and she would conceive a holy seed and her final response was 'LET IT BE UNTO ME ACCORDING TO YOUR WORD'. That was faith speaking.

Mary was not going to debate the Word. Mary was not going to doubt the Word. Mary did not require a sign to believe the Word. Mary was simply going to submit to the Word

Are you going to be a Zacharias or a Mary?

Here is wishing you a MARY CHRISTMAS!

Key Thought: Zacharias doubted the word of the Lord and needed a sign, while Mary believed the word of the Lord.
Intelligent Prayer Point: Pray for faith to believe the word of the Lord and not doubt it.
Support Scriptures: Luke 1:13-18 & Luke 1:26-34

December 25

NOT BORN ON CHRISTMAS DAY

Christ was not born on Christmas day.
For starters, there would not have been shepherds on the hills on the 25th of December around Bethlehem. Historians and Bible scholars agree that Jesus most likely was born between August and October. The Bible gives us no specific date for his birth. But the Bible does emphasize that belief in his fleshy birth is prerequisite to true faith in Christ (1 John 4:1-3). [We could not have His death and resurrection if we did not first have His birth].

I will not bore you with all the history on how the 25th of December was chosen to be the birthdate for Christ but suffice to say that it was an attempt to Christianize pagan celebrations. And even till today, there is still a dynamic tension between what is pagan and what is Christian in Christmas festivities. How do we respond to this?

Some, in learning the not-totally-Christian-roots for the 25th of December as the birthday of Jesus Christ, decide to not have anything to do with the festivities of the day.

Romans 14:5,6 says one esteems one day above another and another all days equal. But, whatever you decide to do, do it unto the Lord. If you choose to celebrate Christmas, do so unto the Lord and if you choose not to, also unto the Lord.

Paul said that he became all things to all men, that he might by all means save some (1 Corinthians 9:22). We must use all means to reach the world for Christ. So, despite the unclear origins of Christmas day we still seize the opportunity of the season to unveil Christ. For us Jesus is the reason for the season.

Whatever your persuasion we must be committed to unveiling Christ to the world so, even in this Christmas season, make sure to share Christ. Merry Christmas!

Key Thought: Christ might not have been born on the 25th of December, but must be exalted everyday.
Intelligent Prayer Point: Pray that Christ be unveiled in this season and beyond.
Support Scriptures: Luke 2:6-8 & Romans 1:16

December 26

KNOWING THE WILL OF GOD

Pilot Text: "For this reason we also, since the day we heard it, do not cease to pray for you, and to ask that you may be filled with the knowledge of His will in all wisdom and spiritual understanding." – Colossians 1:9

The knowledge of the will of God is paramount for successful Christian living. You cannot function successfully as a Christian outside the will of God. The only prayer you can be confident of getting answers to, is that which is in accordance to His will. Even faith only functions in the arena of His will. You cannot use faith to make happen, what is not His will. So, knowing the Will of God becomes vital to the Believer. Paul prayed for the Colossians to be filled with the knowledge of His will in all wisdom and spiritual understanding, as I pray the same for you today.

But how do you know the will of God? This has been the challenge of many a Believer.

His Word is His Will. His Will is His Word. The more knowledge of His Word you have, the more knowledge of His Will is yours. Let's not over complicate knowing the Will of God. HIS WORD IS HIS WILL. HIS WILL IS HIS WORD. He will not contradict His Word. So, in finding the Will of God, start with His Word. Don't complicate it. Simplify it. What does the Word say?

Also know that HIS WILL DOES NOT CONTRADICT HIS CHARACTER. When you understand the character of God, His Will becomes easy to discern. He will not contradict His character or His Word.

Before seeking to know His Will in the big decisions of life, obey the simple dictates of His Will in small things and deciphering His direction in the bigger things will be easier.

Today, I pray that you will be filled with the knowledge of His Will in all wisdom and spiritual understanding.

Key Thought: God's will is known in His Word and His character
Intelligent Prayer Point: Pray for a right discernment of His will for you in every situation.
Support Scriptures: Jeremiah 9:23,24, Philippians 3:10 & 1 John 4:6,7

December 27

I HEAR A SOUND

Pilot Text: "Then Elijah said to Ahab, "Go up, eat and drink; for there is the sound of abundance of rain." – 1 Kings 18:41

With no physical evidence, Elijah said he heard the sound of abundance of rain. He definitely was not hearing with physical ears. He was hearing with the ears of faith. In the realm of faith, hearing precedes seeing. I hear before I see. It is the hearing that will cause you to see.

Today, I have a simple word. Like Elijah heard in that day, I hear a sound too.

I hear the sound of abundance. I hear the sound of increase. I hear the sound of blessing. I hear the sound of supernatural turnaround. I hear the sound of new beginnings. I hear the sound of liftings. I hear the sound of break forth. I hear the sound of new jobs. I hear the sound of your breakthrough.

Somebody is moving up today. Someone is moving from being a nobody to being a somebody. Someone is stepping into the fulfillment of purpose today. From pauper to prince. From weak to strong. From sickness to health. From single to married. From wife to mother. From the background to the foreground. From the tail to the head. From below to above. Things are about to turn in your favor. The lines will fall upon you in pleasant places.

I hear a sound. It is the sound of abundance. I am hearing with the hearing of faith. What do you hear?

Key Thought: To receive your miracle, you must hear with the ears of faith.
Intelligent Prayer Point: Pray that your spiritual ears would be open to hear what the Lord is saying.
Support Scriptures: Isaiah 28:23, Matthew 13:9 & Revelations 2:3

December 28

IMAGINE

Pilot Text: "And the Lord said, Behold, the people is one… and now nothing will be restrained from them, which they have imagined to do." – Genesis 11:6

God said that nothing would be restrained from them, which they imagine to do. This is the power of imagination. Great feats start in the realm of imagination. Whatever you do, don't lose your imagination.

Imagination is the ability to create new ideas, images or concepts, internally, of what is yet to exist. Synonyms for imagination include CREATIVITY, resourcefulness, inventiveness, ingenuity and INNOVATION.

Imagination is your ability to dream. Imagination liberates you from your present constraints. Through your imagination, you can be free from your current prison. Via the eyes of imagination, you can view future possibilities. With imagination, I can go where my feet are yet to sojourn. No matter how buffeted your life might be right now, don't lose your imagination.

Don't stop dreaming. Don't lose your dream. Keep dreaming. It starts with a dream. Dreams still come true. But, before we look at how to actualize your dreams and make your imaginations real, you must first have a fertile imagination. The dream can't come true if it does not exist in the first place.

The men with answers are men with imagination; that refuse to be limited by their present constraints. Activate your imagination. Imagine. Dream again! God the Father, The Dream Maker, is looking for men of faith, who would dream again.

Today, engage the power of imagination and dream your way through. Imagine all the possibilities there are with God.

Key Thought: Engage the power of your imagination to go to the next level.
Intelligent Prayer Point: Decree and declare that your imagination will be ever fertile.
Support Scriptures: Joshua 1:8 Proverbs 23:7, Mark 11:24 & 2 Corinthians 10:5

December 29

INSTANTLY AND PROGRESSIVELY

Pilot Text: "…if anyone is in Christ, he is a new creation; old things have passed away; behold, all things have become new." – 2 Corinthians 5:17

Instantaneously, upon salvation, you became a new creation. You were instantaneously made new on the inside, though nothing changed on the outside.

Instantly made whole on the inside. Instantly seated with Christ in heavenly places. Instantly empowered with the power of the ages to come. Instantly translated out of one kingdom into another. Instantly lifted to another level. Instantly delivered. Instantly made wealthy. Instantly blessed with all spiritual blessings in heavenly places. Instantly… It happened so fast that you will have to spend the rest of your earthly Christian life catching up with what happened in an instant.

Instantly, everything as regards you was settled in heaven, but you are still on the earth. So, what do I do with 'myself' that is still on the earth? You are a spirit, who has a soul and lives in a body. Upon salvation, your spirit is saved and in heaven. But what do you do with the other parts of you still on the earth?

Romans 12:1,2 – "I beseech you …present your bodies a living sacrifice, holy, acceptable to God, which is your reasonable service. And do not be conformed to this world, but be transformed by the renewing of your mind…" Present your body as a living sacrifice. Bring your body under subjection. Renew your mind with the Word of God, so that you would be transformed and not conform to the world or the flesh. So, I am saved instantly in my spirit but saved progressively by the renewing of my mind with the Word of God. Without the renewing of the mind, the new birth remains an internal heavenly affair that is not evident to the world.

I praise God for instant salvation, while I commit to progressive salvation through the renewing of my mind with the Word of God. What about you?

Key Thought: Progressively unveil the new you that was birthed in an instant.
Intelligent Prayer Point: Pray for the emergence of the new you.
Support Scriptures: 2 Kings 5:13,14, Romans 6:14 & 2 Corinthians 7:10

December 30

IS GOD STILL IN CONTROL?

Pilot Text: "Then God said, "Let Us make man in Our image, according to Our likeness; let them have dominion... on the earth." – Genesis 1:26

God is in control. Is this an accurate statement? I risk really stirring the hornet's nest, asking this question. We draw so much consolatory strength and hope from it. But, how can God be in control and such terrible evils still take place in the world?

God delegated authority and responsibility for the earth to man in the beginning. But this was a lease that has an expiry date. Adam gave access to the devil through disobedience. Therefore, the world is under the sway of the will of men and Satan. So, in real time, God is not in control of the world: man is and man has largely allowed Satan access to have his way.

So, Jesus taught us to pray 'let Your will be done and Your kingdom come'. If God's Will would automatically be done, He would not ask us to pray for it to be done. So, God is only in control to the degree that men give Him control. The more you give Him charge of, the more He takes charge of.

However, ultimately in the final day, God is still in control. The earth is the Lord's. God is the ultimate owner and all will come back to Him for final judgment and justice. So, He allows the exercise of our will for the duration of the lease on earth but when the lease is done, all shall be brought to book. God is still in control.

What do you mean when you say God is in control? When I say God is in control, I say so in the areas where I know His control has been invited. When I say God is in control, it is because I am allowing Him express His control through me. The more we submit to His control, the more He is in control. WILL YOU GIVE GOD MORE CONTROL TODAY?

Key Thought: God expresses His control through our invitations and submission.
Intelligent Prayer Point: Invite the Lord to take control in every area of your life.
Support Scriptures: John 10:10, Romans 5:6 & Romans 13:1

December 31

IT'S NOT AN END; IT'S A NEW BEGINNING

Pilot Text: "Remember ye not the former things, neither consider the things of old. Behold, I will do a new thing" – Isaiah 43:18

The year is coming to an end. Is it? Who determines when a year ends and when a new one starts? We mostly operate with the Gregorian calendar worldwide. But did you know that there are many different calendars for different cultures? The Chinese New Year falls between January 21 and February 21. The Jewish New Year is celebrated in autumn. Different calendars for different people

There are also fiscal years. A fiscal year is a financial year. Businesses and many organizations run fiscal years, which do not necessarily correlate with the Gregorian calendar, so the fiscal end of year of an organization can be at anytime of the year. All calendars are attempts to measure and make meaning of progress, in time.

The end of any year forces inevitable assessments and review of where we are and what we have achieved. As important as these reviews and assessments are, be careful not to allow the associated unnecessary depression get to you, refuse to allow acquired feelings stick on you and resist the pressure to make decisions simply because its December. Don't be externally controlled, be internally driven. Walk with God. Rejoice and again, I say rejoice!

Just as different cultures have different calendars and different organizations have different fiscal year ends, you too can determine your personal year-end and when your new year starts. A natural year-end & New Year is your birthday, but even that does not have to be your annual equinox. You determine when! Am I saying ignore the global end of year? Of course not! I am saying get in sync with your God, refuse to be controlled by prevailing external attitudes and see every year-end as not an end but an opportunity for a new beginning. IT'S NOT AN END; IT'S A NEW BEGINNING.

Key Thought: In every ending, there is a new beginning.
Intelligent Prayer Point: Pray to see the new beginnings in every ending.
Support Scriptures: Psalms 1:3, Ecclesiastes 3:1 & Galatians 6:9

www.ingramcontent.com/pod-product-compliance
Lightning Source LLC
LaVergne TN
LVHW041118150826
845673LV00007B/2102

* 9 7 8 1 9 1 6 0 6 8 2 2 3 *